CHAUCER

THE PROLOGUE TO THE

CANTERBURY TALES

NOTES, TRANSLATION AND TEXT

COLES EDITORIAL BOARD

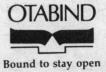

OTABIND

Bound to stay open

Publisher's Note

Otabind (Ota-bind). This book has been bound using the patented Otabind process. You can open this book at any page, gently run your finger down the spine, and the pages will lie flat.

ABOUT COLES NOTES

COLES NOTES have been an indispensible aid to students on five continents since 1948.

COLES NOTES are available for a wide range of individual literary works. Clear, concise explanations and insights are provided along with interesting interpretations and evaluations.

Proper use of COLES NOTES will allow the student to pay greater attention to lectures and spend less time taking notes. This will result in a broader understanding of the work being studied and will free the student for increased participation in discussions.

COLES NOTES are an invaluable aid for review and exam preparation as well as an invitation to explore different interpretive paths.

COLES NOTES are written by experts in their fields. It should be noted that any literary judgement expressed herein is just that — the judgement of one school of thought. Interpretations that diverge from, or totally disagree with any criticism may be equally valid.

COLES NOTES are designed to supplement the text and are not intended as a substitute for reading the text itself. Use of the NOTES will serve not only to clarify the work being studied, but should enhance the reader's enjoyment of the topic.

ISBN 0-7740-3422-X

COLES PUBLISHING COMPANY
TORONTO—CANADA
PRINTED IN CANADA

Manufactured by Webcom Limited
Cover finish: Webcom's Exclusive **Duracoat**

CONTENTS

LIFE OF GEOFFREY CHAUCER 5

THE PILGRIMS 7

CHAUCER AND HIS TIMES 25

CHAUCER'S LANGUAGE 28

CHAUCER'S PRONUNCIATION 29

CHAUCER'S GRAMMAR 30

SYNTAX 33

VOCABULARY 33

VERSIFICATION 36

TRANSLATION AND TEXT 40

NOTES 80

LIFE OF THE AUTHOR

Geoffrey Chaucer, one of the greatest of English writers, made his living as a civil servant and composed poetry as an avocation. His career, however, was such as to contribute to his literary growth. He was born about 1343 of a prosperous family and reared in London. His father, a wine-importer, was able to find him a position (in 1357 or earlier) as a page boy in the household of King Edward III's daughter-in-law, Elizabeth of Ulster; and from this period on, despite the political uncertainties of the age, Chaucer enjoyed the uninterrupted favour of the members of the court of, successively, Edward, Richard II, and Henry IV, both as a man of affairs and as a poet.

He served as a soldier in France in the campaigns of the Hundred Years' War in 1359-1360 and was sent abroad on at least seven occasions between 1368 and 1387, either to France or Italy, on diplomatic missions. He acquired the training necessary for business, probably at the law school known as the Inner Temple. He acted in London as a Controller of Customs from 1374 to 1385, became a Justice of the Peace in Kent in 1385 and a member of Parliament for the county in 1386, served in London again from 1389 to 1391 as a Clerk of the Works, and was thereafter awarded a less active royal appointment as subforester.

He was married (c. 1366) to Philippa Roet of Flanders, who was lady-in-waiting to Queen Philippa and later to John of Gaunt's second wife Constance. (Chaucer's wife's sister became Gaunt's third wife.) Records suggest that he had two sons and a daughter and that his wife died in 1387. He died in 1400 in a house which he had rented in the grounds of Westminster Abbey, and he was buried in that section of the Abbey later to become famous as the Poets' Corner.

The maturation of Chaucer's genius can be illustrated by four works. In the *Book of the Duchess* the poet dreams that he shares the grief of a lonely young knight, who proves to be John of Gaunt mourning his newly lost first wife. The conception is original and the expression of sympathy is gracefully tender, but the framework of the dream-vision and the knight's description of his love are strongly influenced by French models.

In the uncompleted *House of Fame,* another dream-vision, the poet is carried off by an eagle to learn whether those who are in the service of Love are happy or not. The self-confident and domineering eagle was suggested to Chaucer by his reading of Dante's *Paradiso* but here plays a novel comic role in a work which tends to parody the artificiality of medieval courtly love conventions.

In *Troilus and Criseyde,* Chaucer's first major achievement, he amplifies Boccaccio's pseudo-classical romance, *Il Filostrato,* giving depth to the sorrowful Troilus, elusiveness to the timid Criseyde, robust comicality to the officious Pandarus, immediacy to the setting, and a new significance to the tragedy of the two lovers separated by the Trojan War.

In *The Canterbury Tales,* a masterpiece even greater than *Troilus* though uncompleted, Chaucer turned to the English scene, as had his contemporaries Langland and Gower, and excelled all the writers of his era in his delineation of the men, women, children, and animals familiar to him in real life. A richly assorted group of pilgrims entertain themselves by telling stories on the way from London to Canterbury. Through his descriptions in the General Prologue and dramatizations in the links connecting the tales he portrays in detail seven members, of the feudal order, thirteen people associated with religious life, and fourteen townspeople — the chivalrous Knight, the aristocratic Prioress, the fraudulent Pardoner, the impoverished Canon's Yeoman, the amorous Wife of Bath, the reticent civil servant who is Chaucer himself, and the rest who have gained an independent identity as real as that of Falstaff, Tom Jones, or Becky Sharp. And the tales which Chaucer has supplied match the tellers in their rich variety — the Knight's courtly romance, the Miller's racy fabliau, the Second Nun's pious saint's life, the Nun's Priest's mock-heroic fable, the Pardoner's hypocritical sermon, and the Parson's sincere one.

Like most medieval craftsmen, Chaucer, whether as young apprentice or as mature master, followed the pattern of established models; and his success can therefore be partially explained by the vast extent of his reading of "old, approvèd stories." Sources or analogues have been found for almost all of his works and even for his style. His comic tone, for instance, often seems reminiscent of his favorite Latin poet, Ovid; and his philosophical ideas are usually those of Boethius. He appears to have culled materials in turn from the French — from Machaut, Deschamps, Froissart — then from the Italians — from Dante, Petrarch, and Boccaccio — and finally, perhaps, from his fellow countryman Langland. But the ultimate achievements of the medieval master craftsman were profoundly original. Chaucer's skill as a raconteur; his deftness of characterization and description; his perfection in metrical technique; his understanding of man's religious, moral, and philosophical instincts; his knowledge of life and acceptance of its mingled tragedy and comedy; and his transcendent sense of humor are, in combination, unique.

THE PILGRIMS

THE KNIGHT

The Knight is the first of the pilgrims to be introduced. This is doubly appropriate, since the Knight stands at the top of the social hierarchy in this gathering and since he is a virtuous character and embodies a standard of behaviour against which some of the subsequent characters may be judged and found wanting.

Today we look back on knighthood, chivalry, and "curteisye" as romantic and unreal. It is true that few could live up to the rigorous aspirations of the orders of knighthood, yet as a code of behaviour it did exist and Chaucer, who never shows any desire to whitewash or improve his characters, presents the Knight as a real representative of the code. The pope's requirement for these soldiers was that they be "wise, provident, just and pure." They were not only to be champions of the church, but also protectors of the weak, and exemplars of moral virtue.

The list of the places in which the Knight had fought would have a romantic ring to Chaucer's readers. Christendom in the fourteenth century was relatively small, and circumscribed by "heathenesse" — mysterious lands and peoples described by the occasional traveler. Yet the Knight's campaigns are all real enough. They have been divided by historians into three groups, chronologically. The first includes the long struggle to expel the Moorish (Saracen) invaders from Spain.

One source speaks of a challenge issued by the Saracen nobles to the Christian knights to engage in individual combat — possibly a reference to the "lystes" in which the Knight had "slayn his foo." The second group of campaigns ("Alisaundre . . . Lyeys . . . Satalye") occurred in "the Grete See" — the eastern Mediterranean and Asia Minor. King Peter of Cyprus was in command of these, and in preparation he toured all of Europe to secure men, ships, and supplies. Alexandria was a rich and beautiful city, and considered impregnable, but the Christian forces took it, as one source says, "in a massacre unequalled since Pharoah." The third group in which knights from everywhere in Christian Europe were involved took place in "Pruce," "Lettow," and "Ruce," that is to say, on the border of eastern and western Europe. The Teutonic Knights had long been in conflict with the non-Christian peoples to the east. The ceremonial referred to as the "bord" of "Pruce" (52-53) was that of the Teutonic table of honour, a ritual assembly of knights at which those who had acquitted themselves well (like Chaucer's Knight) were placed at the head.

THE SQUIRE

The Knight is a man of maturity and dignity, and by way of contrast, Chaucer now turns to his son the Squire, characterized by youthful enthusiasm. The language suggests his vivid quality: he is "embrouded" with "freshe floures whyte and reede," is represented as "syngynge," and is, in general, "as fresh as is the month of May."

The Squire has had some military experience, but in the main his character is defined in terms of the various accomplishments traditionally expected of the well-born young man. There was, of course, proficiency in horsemanship and combat. The arts of peace were as important as the arts of war. The Squire is skilled in "flotynge" and "daunce." The "daunce" was not unlike the folk dances that we know.

Finally, the reference to the nightingale would be clear to the fourteenth-century reader, since the bird was traditionally associated with love. Like sleepless young men before and since, the Squire was "in hope to stonden in his lady grace."

THE YEOMAN

The position of knight required an attendant squire and a servant as well, which accounts for the Yeoman. In the fifteenth century the term yeoman came to mean a small landholder, but for Chaucer it meant a servant or attendant, in this case with the function of "forster." A "forster" was concerned with game rather than the preservation of the forest, and so the Yeoman wears a "hood of grene" (Lincoln green being the hunter's color) and carries a "sheef of peacock arwes." He has the accoutrements of a hunter (and notice how carefully Chaucer has observed them—the sword and buckler, the dagger, the horn, and of course the "myghty bowe." It was during the fourteenth century that the English longbow (which measured about six feet) replaced the crossbow and the short bow. The longbow delivered an arrow some three hundred yards and it took a strong man to draw and shoot it properly, which was perhaps why bowmanship was a heroic skill in Chaucer's day.

THE PRIORESS

In the presentation of the Prioress we see a kind of poetic technique, that recurs frequently in the Prologue and the Tales. This is irony, which is a way of making apparently simple statements imply more than they actually say. This suggestive implication is a subtle way of both describing a character and commenting on him at the same time. For example, Chaucer says that the Prioress is "charitable and pitous," that is she has the virtues of charity and mercy, to be expected of someone dedicated to a religious life. The illustrations he then gives of her charity and pity concern not other people, but her pets. The "smale houndes" get (Chaucer is careful to point out) the roasted meat, milk, and finest bread that were regarded as delicacies in a society in which a good many people never had enough to eat. It seems a misdirected kind of charity and pity. Although Chaucer never tells us directly, the ironic implication throughout his portrait of the Prioress—her pretentions to aristocratic French, her fashionable manners, her dress—is that despite her holy calling she is more concerned with worldly things than with the spirit. These ironies are fairly amiable, suggesting that Chaucer likes the Prioress despite her little foibles.

Chaucer emphasizes the Prioress' basic femininity, rather than her spiritual qualities, and he does this with a series of allusions that we miss but that a contemporary would catch immediately. These have to do with the heroines of the popular medieval romances, all of whom were described in a series of conventional phrases. Chaucer uses some of them here, such as "ful symple and coy," and he catalogues the Prioress' face (fine nose, small mouth, soft and red, fair forehead, eyes "greye as glas") in the manner of the conventional romances. There were, furthermore, several fourteenth-century romances in which the heroine's name was Eglentyne. The effect, again, is an ironic association of the religious and the worldly, with the suggestion that the Prioress' real nature is closer to the second than to the first. This gives an ambiguous quality to the brooch she wears (160); supposedly the "love" of the inscription refers to the love of God but, with this particular Prioress, we suspect that it might more truly be said to refer to the love of the secular, material world.

Madame Eglentyne, as a nun, probably came from the upper levels of fourteenth-century society. This class characteristic is underlined by Chaucer in several details. Her French is not real French ("of Parys") but that of "Stratford-atte-Bowe," where the Priory of St. Leonard's was situated. The queen's sister spent many years in this priory and it had other aristocratic and courtly associations, and since

French was, or had been, the language of the court it is likely that French was preserved there as a mark of social refinement. Chaucer is careful to let us know that among the pilgrims the Prioress airs her French from time to time.

THE MONK

In Chaucer's representation of the Monk there is the same element of irony as in that of the Prioress. Thus, after outlining in detail the Monk's extremely irreligious activities, Chaucer tells us that "Now certainly he was a fair prelaat." The inconsistency is deliberate, and we find Chaucer frequently writing in this tongue-in-cheek manner.

Two fundamental rules for the conduct of monks in the Middle Ages were the obligation to work and to remain within their cloister. St. Benedict's Rule (mentioned as applying to the Monk's order at 173) is clear about this: "Idleness is an enemy of the soul. Because of this brethren ought to be occupied in manual labour . . . The monastery ought to be so constructed as to contain within it all necessaries . . . so that there be no occasion for monks to wander abroad since this is in no wise expedient for their souls. Chaucer's readers would of course know of this rule, and they would probably also be familiar with St. Augustine's insistence on physical labour: "the blessed Apostle Paul willed the servants of God to work corporal works which should have as their end a great spiritual reward, for this purpose that they should need food and clothing of no man, but with their own hands procure these for themselves . . ." Chaucer notes the special exasperation that the Monk reserves for Augustine's admonition to labour. Why should we "swynken with his handes and laboure/ As Austen bit? . . . Lat Austen have his swynk to him reserved!"

Hunting is the Monk's favourite pastime and he indicates his irritation with those who objected to hunting clergy in a homely and vivid phrase — "He yaf not of that text a pulled hen/ That seith that hunters been nat holy men." Yet the text was a familiar one, both in St. Jerome ("Esau was a hunter and therefore a sinner") and in the writings of John Gower, a friend of Chaucer's. In his highly moral work, Mirror of Man, Gower attacks any monks who "have a horse and saddle, and money to spend . . . For their pleasure these wealthy monks keep falcons and hawks for river fowl, and dogs and horses for hunting the hare . . ." Verbal echoes of this are plain at 189-92. Gower continues on the subject of the wealthy monk's attire: "for vain honour he is clad in a furred cloak. Let the monk be filled with consternation who makes himself handsome for the world, who wears the finest wool furred with costly grey squirrel rather than a hair shirt." Gower's "costly grey squirrel" is the trimming of the Monk's sleeves with "grys' (194), and Chaucer goes on to indicate the lavish nature of the rest of the Monk's costume, the pin "of gold yroght" which fastened his hood, the soft unwrinkled ("couple") boots, and the well-cared-for horse ("in greet estaat"). The passage concludes with one of the chief, and most expensive, delicacies of the day: roast swan.

THE FRIAR

Chaucer's Friar is the longest of the portraits in the Prologue, and this is perhaps because of the difficulty of the task Chaucer has set for himself. He wants to indicate the greed and hypocrisy of a certain class of fourteenth-century cleric, and also create for us an individual who is somehow likeable. Therefore he must balance the many implicit criticisms of the Friar's behaviour with touches that go some way to redeeming him as a "merye" human being whose "eyen twynkled in his heed aryght/ As doon the sterres in the frosty nyght." The treatment of the Friar is mainly in terms of his social function as a member of one of the four orders of begging friars, and we must know something of the history of these orders to understand why Chaucer and other contemporary writers felt it necessary to attack them.

Friars were distinguished from monks in that their task was active service in the world as opposed to the monks' life within the cloister. There were four different orders of friars — the Franciscans, Dominicans, Carmelites, and Augustinian (or Austin) friars — all were begging orders, and all arrived in England during the thirteenth century. Though founded by different men all of the orders, in their early days, had found inspiration in the example of the founder of the Franciscans, St. Francis of Assisi. Since he and his disciples had renounced personal wealth, St. Francis ruled that they might beg for food in times of real hardship and in this way preserve themselves to go on with their work. However the purity and zeal of the saint and his disciples did not survive long after their deaths, and by the fourteenth century the Franciscans had begun to accumulate wealth and power, as had the other begging orders. At about this time criticism of their affluence and their methods of obtaining money had begun, and Gower typifies it when he writes that "it is useless for these evil friars to plead the virtues of St. Francis when they do not follow him in any respect. Although the brethren [i.e., of the different orders] may differ from each other in dress, all are alike in their neglect of their Rule."

As a "lymytour" the Friar was allotted a particular geographical area in which to operate, and here again we see the way St. Francis' original notion of necessary begging had been perverted. There are two lines of the Prologue not given in our text, since they may not be genuine, but they are typical of the sort of thing being said of the friars in the period: "He yaf a certeyne ferme for the graunt/ Noon of his brethren came there in his haunt." "Ferme" is a form of rent, and the meaning is clear enough. The Friar paid for the right to beg in a district, and no other friar could beg in that area. By this time religious begging had become a remunerative occupation.

The begging friars' immorality extended beyond the monopoly of the profitable begging trade. Chaucer's Friar uses "daliaunce and fair language" to ingratiate himself with women, and if these fail there is the more concrete persuasion of "knyves and pynnes" — short, ornamental knives and brooch pins — for the "faire wyves." Scholars generally agree that the reference at 212-13 is to the friars' practice of arranging marriages for women who had been their mistresses.

Late in the thirteenth century the pope had given friars permission to hear confession, and this was much abused. The friar had little interest in penitence; his purpose was to gain a "good pitaunce." We have some of Chaucer's most acid irony at 225-32, when he describes the Friar's view that all the sinner needs to do is to give money to a "poor" order to obtain divine forgiveness. The Friar knows the taverns and barmaids of every town far better than the lepers or beggars.

Chaucer draws attention to the richness of the Friar's dress: "lyk a maister or a pope/ Of double worstede/ was his semycope/ And rounded as a belle out of the presse." Yet despite his corruption and moral laxity, Chaucer maintains the Friar's humanity and even his likeability; this is done in the last few lines, where he is associated with song and enjoyment.

THE MERCHANT

The Merchant would most probably be engaged in the export of wool and hides. Most of this trade occurred between England and the Netherlands, hence the Merchant's concern with keeping the shipping routes open between these two countries, especially since the French were said to be planning an invasion of England.

The Merchant talks "always" of his commercial enterprises, not unlike some businessmen today. Nor is he quite as upright as he seems. The church condemned usury, or the making of money out of money ("eschaunge" being one form of this), and merchants with money to put to work were forced to invent a devious sort of underground transaction ("chevyssaunce"), which was, in effect, lending money at interest. Hence the "dette" that the Merchant is in. As Mr. Rexroth has said, "The Merchant is not hood-winking his creditors; the entire economy which the Merchant represents is founded on debt, called credit today." The Merchant is one of the first examples of the capitalist system of the financing of ventures in commerce by extended loans. This sort of activity was regarded as morally delinquent. One fourteenth-century sermon says that, although God created the clergy, the knights, and the labourers, the devil created usurers, burghers, and merchants.

THE CLERK

The Clerk of Oxenford is not quite a student in our sense of the word, but rather a member of the clergy engaged in advanced studies and one who has never been appointed to a living ("benefice"), or church post with remuneration. There is a suggestion (292) that he is not "worldly" enough to seek and gain such an appointment, and the whole description is based on this notion of dedicated, scholarly unworldliness. The Clerk is, as we would say, doing postgraduate studies. Much of this would be devoted to the works of Aristotle, who occupied a large part of the medieval university curriculum. This sort of extended scholarship was financially difficult, since the scholar had few ways of supporting himself except through gifts (299) and remuneration from the tutoring of junior students — a system already in effect in the fourteenth century and the basis for the colleges (or collection of tutoring scholars) of Oxford and Cambridge. The "twenty bookes" of Aristotle (294) means little to us today unless we recall the rarity and price of books at the time. To Chaucer's readers this library represents a tremendous financial sacrifice on the part of the Clerk.

Students are not now, and were not then, as austere as Chaucer's Clerk. Contemporary records speak of the traditional student pleasures, and gaiety, and even (at Oxford) violence. The Clerk of the Prologue is devoted to learning, and the little he does say is "sownynge in moral vertu." Physically he is austere. His horse is lean as a rake, "And he was nat right fat, I undertake." We think, by contrast, of the fat Monk and his well-fed mount, as Chaucer intends us to. There is no question of irony or satire in the description of the Clerk. Chaucer respects him without qualification and has given to him the simplest, finest, and briefest eulogy that any scholar-teacher has ever had: "And gladly wolde he lerne and gladly teche."

THE SERGEANT OF THE LAW

Do not confuse the term "Sergeant" as Chaucer uses it here with modern noncommissioned military rank. In the fourteenth century it designated a special order of barristers, or lawyers, who were selected by the reigning monarch and from whose ranks the common law judges were chosen until 1890, when the order was abolished. The sergeants of the law were on the same social level as knights and the sons of noblemen. In Chaucer's time there were only about two dozen of them in the whole of England.

Chaucer does not question his lawyer's ability, or his knowledge of the law. Since English law is largely "case law," in which precedents direct particular judgments, a lawyer's knowledge of previous decisions must be extensive. Yet the statement that the lawyer knows all the "doomes" (judgments) since William the Conqueror is another example of Chaucer's deliberate exaggeration — we are to infer that he talked as though he knew them all. Chaucer's attitude toward the lawyer becomes explicit at 321-22, and here again the criticism is universally valid; we still have with us those who are anxious to give the impression that they are constantly involved in matters of great import, who "seem busier than they are."

Chaucer subtly suggests the lawyer's failings. He is "war and wys," but it is his cunning, not his goodness, that is emphasized. He is rich (a great "purchasour"), but this is through sharp legal practice. Many of Chaucer's contemporaries denounced lawyers for promoting legal conflicts, bribing those who gave evidence and using the law to get control of lands.

THE FRANKLIN

It is significant that the Sergeant of Law should be travelling in the company of the Franklin. The lawyer would choose no ordinary member of society as his companion and the Franklin, as Chaucer makes very clear, was a substantial person in every way. He presided at sessions of justices of the peace (355), had been a member of parliament (356, the "knyght" was the representative of the "shire"), and had been a sheriff and a treasurer (359).

One of the first things we learn about the Franklin is that "Of his complexion he was sangwyn," a phrase which carried a much more elaborate meaning to the fourteenth-century reader than it does to us.

Medieval medical science classified people according to the "humour," or fluid, which was dominant in them. A person's quality or temperament depended upon the way these fluids, or humours, were mixed in him. Thus a dominance of black bile, which corresponds to earth, made a man dull and melancholic.

The word sanguine is derived from the word blood, and the Franklin's character was dominated by the humour of blood. This was understood to produce several qualities — generosity, kindness, a large appetite, and pleasure in physical satisfaction in general. So the word "sangwyn," which to us simply means of a reddish complexion, contained a whole character analysis for Chaucer's readers, and the account of the Franklin is simply an elaboration of that character.

Much of the elaboration has to do with the Franklin's love for food and the amplitude of his larder ("It snewed in his hous of mete and drynke.").

THE GUILDSMAN

Chaucer's five guildsmen come from different crafts yet wear the same uniform, so that they must belong to a parish rather than a craft guild. These originated in the practicing members of a parish joining together to suport a priest to perform various religious functions for them, but they soon developed into powerful associations with many other functions, at first social and benevolent, and later political. They were an important social force, and certainly "a solempne and greet fraternitee."

Chaucer tells us that each of his guildsmen seemed "a fair burgeys," able to sit on the dais of a guildhall. Since only the mayor and aldermen were allowed to do this, Chaucer probably means only to imply that each of them was worthy of the rank of alderman, "for the wisdom that he kan." Certainly their wives thought they were (374). In a sly aside (375-78), Chaucer touches on that wifely trait which is a universal rather than a specifically medieval thing. The suggestion is that the ambition to be alderman on the part of his characters is inspired in a large part by their wives' desire to be styled "lady" or "madame" and head the procession at the "vigilies".

THE COOK

The guildsmen are at least substantial enough to be able to bring their own cook with them on the pilgrimage to Canterbury. Brief though it is, the account makes him an individual, a competent cook with a "mormal" on his shin who could "knowe a draught of London ale." According to the physicians of the day, the ulcerous "mormal" was the direct result of "the eating of melancholic foods and the drinking of strong wines."

THE SHIPMAN

The Shipman — the master of the Madelaine — represents an occupation rapidly gaining in importance in Chaucer's day. Seagoing activities were increasing and from the fourteenth century on; the sea, and those who sailed on it, would be vital to England's interests. The Shipman is presented as a rough-and-ready character ("Of nyce conscience took he no keep") as anyone in his position was obliged to be. The seas were the scene of a good deal of international piracy. There was as yet, in England, only a small national maritime force — "the King's ships," as they were called — and therefore the individual merchantmen traveled armed, ready either to repel attack or, on occasion, to initiate it. The men of the west country ports, such as Dartmouth, had been issued what amounted to a royal license for privateering against England's seagoing enemies, in part to protect English trade, in part to enrich themselves.

The Shipman is immediately identified by his inability to ride; the phrase "as he kouthe" (390) might be more fully translated as "insofar as he was able to do it at all." We must also suppose that "certeinly he was a good felawe" (395) is in some degree ironic, since it is immediately followed by an account of the way in which the Shipman steals wine from the "chapman," or merchant, who was paying him to convey and protect it. The Shipman's easy conscience extends to more than wine-stealing. When victor in combat at sea, he unburdens himself of his prisoners by making them walk the plank — "By water he sente them hoom to every land."

THE DOCTOR OF PHYSIC

Medical knowledge was a combination of what had been inherited from the ancients and a good deal of folk knowledge of botanical and herbal cures. The degree of Doctor of Physic took as long to get in the 14th century as it does today, and included the knowledge of astrology and the influence of the stars on human affairs and especially the individual's health. To Chaucer's contemporary readers the necessity of a physician's expert knowledge of astronomy was as obvious as to us the indispensibility of a surgeon's grounding in anatomy. For the doctor's remedies had to be administered at the proper planetary hours. And those were the hours at which the constitution of the patient and the constitution of a sign or planet were in due correspondence.

THE WIFE OF BATH

The Wife of Bath is one of Chaucer's most famous characters. He makes her a vivid presence here in the Prologue, and enlarges the portrait later in The Canterbury Tales in her own prologue to her own tale. The geographical notation "biside Bathe" is not as vague as it sounds. It meant the small parish just outside the north gate of Bath called "St. Michael-without-the-walls," and it was probably at the door of St. Michael's church that the Wife's many marital encounters took place.

The Wife's great talent is for cloth-making, and we get Chaucer's tongue-in-cheek touch again when he asserts her superiority over the cloth-makers "of Ypres and of Gaunt," an opinion that we suspect came straight from the Wife herself. There follows an illuminating little touch concerning her character. No woman in the parish, Chaucer says, ought to precede the Wife to the "offrynge" in church. And if any did "certeyn so wrooth was she/ That she was out of alle charitee." We can well imagine it, and so the tone is set for the development of this boisterous, egotistical, but fundamentally very likeable character later in the Tales.

Two points are made about the Wife: her amorous nature and her habit of going on pilgrimages. The reference to the husbands "at chirche dore" is explained by the fact that medieval marriages were performed at the entrance of the church; since most of the service was not in Latin, the wedding group proceeding inside afterward for the nuptial mass. But the striking thing about the line is the number of mates the Wife has had. In part the reason is economic — the Wife is a woman of property and the possessor of a commercially valuable skill. The Middle Ages were more romantic in their literature than in life, and just as a dowerless woman found it difficult to get married, so one with money found it easy. But the main reason for the many marriages is simply that the Wife enjoyed the company of men. Chaucer goes on to suggest the "oother compaignye in youthe," but gallantly refuses, in the next line (462), to elaborate on the Wife's premarital liaisons. How would a woman of the Wife's ebulient and garrulous nature ("wel koude she laughe and carpe") get on in marriage? Here we are told that she is "somdel deef," but later in the

Tales we discover that this is because her fifth husband once became so infuriated with her that he beat her about the head and impaired her hearing.

There is no real inconsistency in a woman of the Wife's worldly nature going on a series of pilgrimages to holy shrines. By the fourteenth century the pilgrimage had become for some a social excursion as well as a religious act, a fact reflected in some of Chaucer's other less-than-devout pilgrims. Some of the contemporary writers complain of married women going on pilgrimages, and it may well have been a device for escaping the restrictions imposed by a husband. Jerusalem was, of course, the principal destination for pilgrimages. The Wife has been there three times, where she would have been shown the white stone on which the True Cross stood, and near which the first crusaders were buried. She has also been to Rome, where the major pilgrim attractions were St. Peter's (a visit there procuring many years of pardon), and St. Paul's Cathedral, where the stone on which St. Paul was beheaded was said to cure the sick and maimed who touched it.

THE PARSON

Most of the figures in The Canterbury Tales (and in the tales they tell) have the normal portion of human failings and some of them a good deal more than the normal, but the Parson is a study in virtue. One of the reasons for this lies in the other clerics — notably the Pardoner and the Summoner — who are thoroughly corrupt. It was Chaucer's intention to delineate the failings of individual people, not the institution they happened to be part of, and in the creation of the good Parson he tells us by implication that the church does have servants who faithfully carry out its commands. The Parson is in some ways a parallel to the Knight, the latter exhibiting virtue in the secular world as the former does in the ecclesiastical. One effect of this somewhat special treatment is to make the Parson a little less solid as a character than the other pilgrims. Since Chaucer is mainly concerned with the Parson's virtuous qualities, he does not provide those sharply observed details of appearance or habits of speech and action that render the others so vividly.

One abuse which was rife in the Middle Ages among clerics is implied by the Parson's refusal to "cursen" — that is, to excommunicate — those who did not pay their tithes. Chaucer's Parson not only does not use this threat, but aids his parishoners from the general "offryng," or collection, and even from his own "substance."

The major virtue that Chaucer attributes to his Parson is that he practices what he preaches: "first he wroghte, and afterward he taughte." The members of any religious hierarchy are always especially vulnerable to the charge that there is a discrepancy between what they teach and what they themselves do. The obligation to be a normal leader puts them in a special position, which Chaucer sums up in a line which has become part of the language's store of proverbs: "That if gold ruste, what shal iren do?" Another contemporary abuse is glanced at in the next passage (507-12). This is clerical absenteeism, which usually took the form of serving in one of the especially endowed chantries in the city (many of which were set up by the guilds) while simply abandoning the rural parish, or hiring a substitute. This had the advantages of increasing the cleric's finances, since the city chantries and foundations were usually wealthy, and also of avoiding the rigorous life of the country parish.

There are some scholars who believe that Chaucer's Parson is meant to be a representative of that group of fourteenth-century religious reformers who were followers of John Wycliffe (1320-84). They were called Lollards (the name was suposed to represent the mumbling delivery of their sermons), and they attacked the church's wealth and advocated the poverty of the clergy. The Parson himself never supports these arguments, but probably Chaucer agreed with some of the Lollard views.

THE PLOWMAN

The Plowman is the Parson's brother, and the connection is made deliberately, since they both represent the virtues of their respective occupations. Chaucer probably does not here reflect the general view of the upper classes toward the peasantry. The Canterbury Tales was begun in 1386 (or '87), and the Peasants' Revolt had taken place in 1381. There was still a good deal of bitterness about the slaughter of these citizens of London whom the rioting peasants regarded as being responsible for their economic plight. As a justice of the peace and a member of parliament, Chaucer might be expected to share the views of the upper class. It is a tribute to his artist's ability to transcend political issues that he gives so admiring an account of a representative of the peasantry. The Plowman's virtues are like his brother: simple and issuing in action. His creed is also simple; in fact, it is the basic obligation of his religion: "God loved he best . . . And thanne his neighebore right as hymselve."

THE MILLER

Of the lines devoted to the Miller, notice how many are concerned with physical appearance rather than with more abstract qualities.

The opening suggestion of "stout carl" and "Ful big he was of brawn" is carried on in what follows: he is short-armed, broad, a "thikke knarre" with a red spade beard, and even the wart on his nose, with its "tuft of herys/ Rede as the bristles of a sowes erys" is specified. The general effect is of robust physique — compare, for example, the Clerk, who Chaucer says looks hollow.

Millers were most important in the medieval economy and we hear must about them in the stories, poems, and documents of the period. Like Chaucer, many of these sources refer to the millers' dishonesty and sharp practice. The tenants of any manor were obliged to use their lord's mill, and that was operated by the miller, who was thus in an excellent position to cheat them. This is what Chaucer's Miller does, stealing the flour that should be theirs and getting his fee for milling three times over. It is easy to see how the ironic expression concerning the miller's "thombe of gold" arose, and it probably carries a double significance: that millers were wealthy and that they used a heavy thumb on the scales, to make it seem that they were giving more flour than they were.

Prof. W. C. Curry has examined the way in which the Middle Ages interpreted character according to physiognomy. The fourteenth-century reader would be able to deduce the Miller's character from his physical description. Someone of the Miller's thick-set build was held to be immodest and talkative, as well as violent and easily angered; the flaring nostrils indicate lust; the large mouth ("a greet forneys") means a liar, as well as one much given to profanity. Yet Chaucer is lenient with the Miller, whose sins are venial ones.

THE MANCIPLE

While Manciples might be attached to various kinds of institutions, they were most commonly employed by colleges or the Inns of Court, which were very like colleges, since their members were students of the law. This is the point of Chaucer's pretended surprise at 574-75 that such a "lewed" (unlearned) man should be so much more acute than the "heap of lerned men" who were his masters. Chaucer is really contrasting the shrewd practical knowledge of the Manciple with what we can suppose to be the relative naivete of the young legal scholars.

The Manciple was obliged to be shrewd. His duties included accounting for the foodstuffs in the kitchen and buttery, keeping the accounts, and supervising the kitchen and the cook. This last may account for a quarrel that occurs later in the Tales between the Manciple and the Cook. Given their working relationship, there was probably a tradition of dislike between them, which Chaucer dramatized.

Chaucer's treatment of the Manciple is relatively flat and colourless, and we neither admire nor disapprove of him. He is a figure reduced to his various functions, not a study in character.

THE REEVE

Although we do not get as extensive a physical description of the Reeve as we did of the Miller, there is enough details, according to Prof. Curry, to give the contemporary reader some notion of his personality. The Reeve is a "sclendre colerik man," which accords with the belief that those who were thin were also of a choleric humor, easy to anger. But thin people were also held to be sharp-witted, and with excellent memories, and we can see how such qualities would go with the kind of double-dealing the Reeve engages in — no audit could catch him out, and he remembers the mistakes of all his staff. The long legs "Ylik a staf" were evidence of lustfulness, and while this trait does not appear in the Prologue, it does emerge in the tale he tells later in the work.

For us the character of the Reeve is sharp, doubtlessly able to be unpleasant, and endlessly intent on the shrewd and gainful exploitation of his job. It is suggested that he has held this position for a long time (601), and that everything of his lord's is "hoolly in this Reves governyng." He is efficient ("Wel koude he kepe a gerner and a bynne") and it is suggested that he is dishonest in his accounts, yet "Ther was noon auditour koude on him wynne," i.e., no one could catch him out. It is also significant that he knew and remembered all the particular failings of those working beneath him and let them know that he knew. They would never reveal any of his misappropriations and were in fact "adrad of hym as of the deeth." The Reeve is daring in his dishonesties. He has the temerity (or his lord, Chaucer may be implying, has the stupidity) to lend the lord what is really the lord's own property, for which he receives "a thank, and yet a cote and hood."

There is another point of interest about the Reeve, and that is his connection with the Miller. Both are memorably described by Chaucer. One leads the procession of pilgrims, the other stays at the end of it. They are sharply contrasted in appearance, one short and thick, the other long and thin. Later in The Canterbury Tales they have a violent falling-out. The Miller's Tale enrages the Reeve, since it seems to be an attack on him, and he attacks the Miller in his own tale. It also becomes clear that they had known one another before the meeting at the Tabard. This may, of course, be all Chaucer's invention, and it is true that millers and reeves were traditional antagonists, being rivals for power on the estates. Yet Chaucer is so specific about the Miller, and so informative about the Reeve (giving his name, the town he comes from, and even a description of his dwelling), that he may have had two historical characters in mind, and the Miller-Reeve quarrel may have actually occurred, making a topical reference the late fourteenth-century reader would recognize at once.

THE SUMMONER

The introduction of the Summoner begins with a visual description, but there is more to this than simple visualization. Chaucer presents his physical disorders in a way which suggests inner or spiritual corruption. Chaucer was well versed in medical lore, as we saw in his account of the Doctor, and he chooses the Summoner's ailments with the contemporary medical explanations of them in mind. The medieval diagnosticians were very prone to list all diseases of the skin under leprosy, but the cause of the Summoner's condition is given as drunkeness and excessive eating in youth, the "fleshlye liking" of a diseased woman, and "too hot meates, as long use of strong pepper, or garlike, and of unclean wine . . ." Chaucer suggests all these gastronomic excesses at 634-35, where he speaks of "garlek, oynons . . . strong wyn reed as blood," and the Summoner's lechery at 652, where the phrase "a fynch . . . koude he pulle"; actually, "to pull a finch," is a fourteenth-century expression meaning to have sexual relations.

Having indicated in this visual way the diseased nature of the Summoner, Chaucer passes on to his behaviour. When he is drunk he speaks nothing but Latin, but we find that in contrast to the learning of the Clerk and the Parson he knows only "two or thre" terms and those are learned as a bird might learn, by rote. The familiar Latin tag meaning "What law applies?" was "al his philosophie." Then follows the Summoner's abuse of his ecclesiastical office. He permits licentious behaviour (for a price) and indulges in it himself. Although summoners had originally only brought the charge to accused individuals, during the fourteenth century they began to take on some of the function of investigators, or spies, serving the bishop and archdeacon. It is this aspect of their position that leads to the extortionary practices which are denounced by many of the contemporary writers. Excommunication ("Ercedekenes curs") might be performed for a wide variety of sins, such as nonpayment of tithes, sacrilege, desecration, slander, fraud, witchcraft, and so on. It was comparatively easy to indict someone with as inclusive a list as this, which conferred considerable power on the summoner. How Chaucer's Summoner used his power is suggested at 655-60, where the archdeacon's "curs" is either lifted, or never pronounced, because of a payment of money.

As a final touch the Summoner's headgear is as large as an ale-house sign, and his "bokeler" is a huge loaf of bread. These symbols of physical appetite do not suggest robust health (as with the Franklin) but appetite which runs to gluttony.

THE PARDONER

The Pardoner turns out to be a fitting companion for the Summoner and so they join in song. The song the Pardoner sings is a popular love-ditty, but it has been suggested by some scholars that Chaucer gives it to him because of his effeminate nature and that he sings it to the Summoner. This view is to some degree supported by Prof. Curry's findings concerning the medieval view of physiognomy and character. The Pardoner's hair, "yellow as wex" and "smothe" indicates lack of virility, effeminacy of mind, and also deception. However, the effeminacy here may simply be the Pardoner's concern for his clothes and his wish to be in the new mode of fashion. The bright eyes of 684 were supposed to be a sign of folly and immodesty.

The medieval pardoner has as his main occupation the selling of indulgences (the remission of punishment to a repentant sinner), but he might also sell religious relics and preach. The sale of indulgences was an abused practice and finally came to have little to do with the contrition of the sinners. Indulgences were of varying degrees and sold for various prices. Although the money gained through them was meant to be returned to the church, it was obviously easy to adjust the indulgence prices so that not all the money received need be turned in. In addition to this, the people, and especially the simple people, saw the indulgences as a new and easy method of obtaining the remission of sins, and their increased demand increased the pardoner's price. The Pardoner here, with his wallet "Bretful of pardon, comen from Rome al hoot," could expect to do an impressive amount of business in the small English parishes.

The practice of selling religious relics was another notorious abuse. Theose pardoners who sold false religious objects, vowing that they were real, and kept the money were denounced in a papal edict in 1390. Chaucer makes his Pardoner's wares seem particularly exaggerated. A pillowcase becomes "Oure Lady veyl," while a piece of canvas is St. Peter's sail "when that he wente/ Upon the see." The "pigges bones" would presumably be peddled as the remains of a saint. Chaucer recounts this with the simple wonder he sometimes affects — "Ne was ther swich another pardoner" — but his meaning is clear, and when we get to the phrase "a noble ecclesiaste" the harsh irony is apparent. Finally there is the Pardoner's facility in song and preaching, which, as a thorough-going confidence man, we might have expected him to have. Here again we note the perversion of the rites of the church, the "lesson" and the "offertorie" used in order "To wynne silver, as he ful wel koude." A contemporary statement (1414) will serve to show the attitude of the reformers within the church to the practices of the pardoners: "Whereas the shameless pardoners sell Indulgences and squander their gains in disgraceful fashion with the prodigal son: but what is more detestable they preach pubiicly, and pretend falsely that they have full powers of absolving both living and dead alike from punishment and guilt, along with other blasphemies, by means of which they plunder and seduce the people, and drag them down with their own person to the infernal regions of affording them frivolous hope and an audacity to commit sin: therefore let the abuses of this pestilential sect be blotted out from the threshold of the Church."

THE HOST

The Host (whose name, we discover later, is Harry Bailly) does not really come into his own until the telling of tales begins, but his character is suggested here. He is a large, commanding, genial man. His manner is direct and sensible, he is efficient, and, Chaucer says, he is fit "For to been a marchal in an halle." This is high praise, since "an halle" is a lord's manor, where the marshal served as the household's chief organizer for the guests and their food and drink. There is evidence to suggest that Chaucer is praising a real innkeeper here, since a Harry Bailly did keep an inn in Southwark in Chaucer's time. The Subsidy Roll of Southwark for 1380-81 records one "Henricus Bailiff, Ostyler," and there are several other references to him in various other connections.

The Host's importance in the Prologue lies in his proposal to the pilgrims that they entertain themselves on the journey to Canterbury and back by telling tales. After seeing to his guests "vitaille" and "wyn" (and also attending to the "reckenynges," for he is always a practical man) he explains the terms of his proposal. It calls for a hundred and twenty tales, since each pilgrim is to tell two stories on the journey to Canterbury and two more on the way back to Southwark, where the teller of the best tale is to be given dinner at the cost of all ("Here in this place" he adds, still practical). Through the host, Chaucer has proposed an immense narrative task for himself that was never finished. Of the one hundred and twenty tales only twenty were completed, seven of the thirty pilgrims tell no tales at all, and we part with the pilgrimage before it reaches Canterbury. This simply means that the Prologue (as we might expect) was written before any, or very many, of the tales were completed.

We notice how pleasantly, yet at the same time how deftly and with what command, the Host takes over the direction of the pilgrims. There is no debate about his plan. Those who want to "stonden at my juggement," he says, "Hoolde up youre hondes withouten moore speche" — and they do. From this point on in The Canterbury Tales the host will be chairman, stage manager, judge, and choric commentator for the group's succession of fictional recitals. Now he arranges the drawing of lots to decide who will tell the first story. Does he 'arrange' the choice of the Knight? Certainly he is capable of it, and Chaucer leaves the matter in doubt (843-44).

CHAUCER AND HIS TIMES

HIS WORLD

The technological differences between our age and Chaucer's are obvious enough when we think of the weird astrological-medical theories of the "Doctour of Phisik" (*Prologue* 411-44), or of the fact that it took Chaucer's pilgrims three days of hard travel to traverse the sixty miles between London and Canterbury. The differences in society and its assumptions are important in understanding the actions and attitudes of Chaucer's pilgrims.

The social structure of England (and all Europe) in the fourteenth century was feudal, that is to say power radiated from the king, through his nobles (when he could control them), and through their subjects, with little kingly power reaching the lower echelons of society. The king and his nobles owned the land, which was divided into great agricultural estates, and these provided the men, material, and money which supported the crown and its wars. Society was organized in a hierarchical form, one's wealth and power being a matter of what position one occupied on the hierarchical ladder. This ladder extended from the king, through the great noblemen-landlords (like Chaucer's patron, John of Gaunt, Duke of Lancaster), down through lesser landlords and their various executive officers with, at the bottom, the serfs who worked the land for their masters. It is perhaps important to note that while we may regard this system as unjust and oppressive, the medieval people could conceive of no other. Each level of society had its rights and privileges, and each had its duties and obligations. Despite the occasional abuse they regarded the system as right and proper.

Three groups of Chaucer's pilgrims may be isolated to suggest how this system worked. The first represents agricultural feudalism (the first and basic kind) founded on land ownership and service. The Knight, who is highest on the scale, is a landowner, and has therefore served in the wars for his king, and he will be followed in this by his son, the Squire. The Knight's Yeoman is a servant, whose only duty is to the Knight. The Franklin also holds land, perhaps "in fee" from some noble, but more probably in his own right. His service is the direction of his farm, his obligation to the noble or king being doubtless in the form of the yearly harvest, and of men in time of need. The Miller does not himself own land but has been given the right to mill all grain on an estate; the Reeve manages an estate. They are both servants, but of an exalted kind, and make shrewd and profitable use of their power, as we shall see. The lowest in the hierarchy is the Plowman, who simply tills the land.

England was changing in the fourteenth century, and one of the most important changes was the growth of a new, urban society (mainly in London) where the feudal structure was somewhat modified. Neither the Doctor nor the Sergeant of the Law owned land, although they were both men of substance. The Doctor (Chaucer tells us) made money out of the plague, and the Lawyer made money out of almost everything. They were the beginning of a new class, today called professional men. The Manciple and the Merchant and even the Wife of Bath (who is a clothmaker) also represent the urbanization process. They were not directly commanded by anyone, and in time they became the mercantile middle class who overthrew the monarchy and the last vestiges of feudalism in the civil war of the seventeenth century. It is also significant that the Haberdasher, the Carpenter, the Weaver, and the Dyer are presented together, in that they are all members of one of the great parish guilds. It was through these craft and parish guild associations that the new urban artisans achieved the power that they lacked through not belonging to the land-hierarchy.

There is yet a third group, constituting a kind of feudal system of its own, and representing one of the most powerful elements of medieval society — the church. Nine of Chaucer's thirty pilgrims belong to the clergy, and it would be difficult to overestimate the importance of the Roman Catholic church to the lives of the people of western Europe in the fourteenth century. They might disregard its teaching (as some of the pilgrims do) or complain of its abuses (as Chaucer does) but from baptism, through confirmation and marriage, to the funeral rites, it was intimately connected with their lives. It was a visibly potent force throughout England, from the great cathedrals — such as Canterbury — and the religious houses, down to the humble parish churches.

Despite the worldly aspects of life that so often appear in *The Canterbury Tales* we should not forget that the people Chaucer gathers together are pilgrims, and that the occasion for their gathering is the spring pilgrimage to the shrine of "the holy blisfil martir," St. Thomas Becket, at Canterbury. We can gauge the importance of the church in men's lives by noting how many varieties of belief or simulated belief Chaucer presents. They run all the way from the dedicated holiness of the Parson, through the superficial observances of the Prioress, to the outright hypocrisy of the Summoner and Pardoner. Chaucer, looking about him, sees fit to define a large proportion of his characters by where they stand with regard to the church.

It is sometimes suggested that the medieval world was a happier, simpler, and less troubled time than our own. In some ways this is true — certainly Chaucer's pilgrims are free from many of our modern anxieties — yet the fourteenth century had its own troubles, and it is an oversimplification to regard it as a time of innocent good humour. In fact it is the overall good humour of Chaucer's treatment that has fostered this view, and while he is basically optimistic, he would be unlikely to accept it.

The plague, or Black Death (to which Chaucer occasionally alludes) entered England in mid-century with dreadful consequences. It is said that half the population was wiped out, and while this may be an exaggeration, it is no exaggeration to say that medieval man lived in constant fear of its ravages. One of the effects of the plague was to inflate prices and further depress the already grim living conditions of those at the bottom of the economic ladder. This in turn produced the insurrection known as the Peasants' Revolt (1381), in which the infuriated mob murdered a good many of those whom they regarded as their exploiters. Chaucer — as a justice of the peace and a member of parliament — might be expected to be bitter about this unprecedented attack on the social order. It may be a measure of his magnanimity that only a few years after the rebellion his portrait of the Plowman in the *Prologue* is remarkable for its praise of the peasant virtues.

The Hundred Years War continued, with the French threatening to invade England; this is one of the reasons for the war-like nature of Chaucer's Shipman, whose merchant ship was obliged to be a fighting vessel, and it also accounts for the Merchant's anxiety about trade if the shipping route between Middleburg in the Netherlands and Orwell in England is broken.

The church itself was divided at the time, one faction having a pope at Rome and the other at Avignon, with some of Europe (including England) supporting the first and some (including Scotland) the second. The confusion resulting from this situation was probably in part the cause of the clerical abuses that produced so much complaint (some of it in the *Canterbury Tales*) during the period.

If we set these disruptions alongside the achievements of art and literature, the security of a stable society, and the calm that comes from faith (the qualities usually presented as typical of the Middle Ages), we shall probably be somewhere near the truth. At any rate it was a time of transition and great variety: an appropriate time for the creation of a work as varied and multicolored as *The Canterbury Tales.*

CHAUCER'S LANGUAGE

The language which Chaucer wrote and spoke is different from modern English, and we must therefore make an initial effort to familiarize ourselves with it. The scholars of our day call the language of Chaucer's age, in retrospect, Middle English, thereby differentiating it both from its ancestor, Old English or Anglo-Saxon, spoken before 1066, and from its descendant, our modern English, spoken after 1500. But Chaucer, we must remember, would have considered *his* language normal, modern English. And he would have had every right to do so, for his particular dialect, among the diverse regional and class dialects of England, was that spoken by the educated classes of London during the fourteenth century, and it later became the model for standard modern English when other dialects began to lose prestige.

Unfortunately for the subsequent appreciation of his work, however, language is ever changing. Consciously or unconsciously, speakers effect minor innovations within the limited sets of distinctive sounds, intonations, grammatical forms, sentence patterns, and words currently in use; and in time the subtle balance within these sets of interdependent speech elements is changed so that the language of yesterday seems unnatural or obscure. The changes which the English language underwent, particularly in its pattern of contrasting sounds, were remarkably extensive in the century after Chaucer's death in 1400. Our conservative and arbitrary English spelling system affords a most inadequate clue to the actual facts, but, presumably, if Chaucer had reappeared in the age of Shakespeare, two centuries later, Elizabethans would have found his speech almost incomprehensible, not merely because he used some words that had become archaic but particularly because an extensive shift of vowel sounds had rendered the still surviving words and grammatical forms which he used unrecognizable in sound. By contrast, three and a half centuries after the death of Shakespeare, we ourselves should find the English spoken in the Elizabethan age still intelligible.

By a process of ingenious deductions from the mute and ambiguous written records of Chaucer's language, scholars have established the principal features of sound, intonation, form, arrangement, and vocabulary characteristic of the language actually spoken in his time. The following simplified account of these findings offers a practical working guide for those who wish to understand what Chaucer wrote and to read his poetry aloud in somewhat the manner in which the poet himself would have read it. No hypothetical reconstruction can be absolutely correct in all its details; but, if we are to appreciate the flavour of an author's language, whether we are reading Chaucer's poetry or Burn's lyrics or the tales of Uncle Remus, some sort of imaginative projection into a dialect other than our own is necessary.

CHAUCER'S PRONUNCIATION

To transform the written transcript of Chaucer's language consistently into spoken words, the first requirement is a readjustment of our sense of relationship between spelling symbols and spoken sounds.

(1) Pronounce all written consonants as we do those in modern English. However, *gh* as in *night,* though now silent, was pronounced like the *ch* in the Scottish pronunciation of *loch* or in the German pronunciation of *Bach.* This unfamiliar sound is like the initial sound in modern English *how* but more strongly breathed.

(2) Pronounce all the syllables in a word, even those which are represented only by a final *–e* and are no longer pronounced in modern English. Thus, pronounce Chaucer's *dame* with two syllables

as *dah-meh,* and his *dames* as *dah-mess.* This final unstressed vowel probably had the same sound as the final unstressed vowel, when unemphatic, in modern English *Stella* or *raven.*

It is most important for our understanding of Chaucer's metres to note that, as in classical French poetry, all final syllables were pronounced, including those ending in *–e, –ed, –en, –es, –eth.*

(3) Pronounce all written vowels according to their so-called "Continental" values, that is, according to the sounds which they represent in modern French or Italian, or in our modern pronunciation of Latin.

Thus, pronounce the vowel spelled *a* in Chaucer's *dame* as the *ah* sound of modern French *dame* (or modern English *father*), not as the *ay* sound of modern English *dame.* Other instances are Chaucer's *bare, care, fame, game, hate, lame, make, name, page, rage, save, take, wake.*

Pronounce the vowel spelled *e* or *ee* in Chaucer's *regioun* as the *ay* sound of modern French *région* (or modern English *able*), not as the *ee* sound of modern English *region.* Other instances are Chaucer's *be, me, thee.* There are a large number of exceptions in this case, but the important fact to remember is that Chaucer's *e* is never pronounced as the *ee* sound of modern English *region, be,* and so on.

Pronounce the vowel spelled *i* or *y* in Chaucer's *fine* as the *ee* sound in modern French *fine* (or modern English *machine*), not as the *eye* sound in modern English *fine.* Other instances are *bite, glide, kynde* (modern English *kind*), *mine, prime, ride, strive, thine, wyn* (modern English *wine*).

Pronounce the vowel spelled *ou* or *ow* in Chaucer's *doute* as the *ou* sound in modern French *doute* (or modern English *soup*), not as the *ow* sound in modern English *doubt*), *foul, hous, mous, tour* (modern English *tower*), *out.*

The vowels represented by *o, u,* and diphthongs diverge less notably from modern usage and need not be described here.

CHAUCER'S GRAMMAR

The grammatical forms used by Chaucer are less troublesome for the modern reader than the now-vanished pronunciation, for contrasting forms can be positively identified from the written record, and most of them survive, at least as archaisms, in modern English.

NOUNS

The numerous declensional systems derived from the earliest stages of the English language had by the time of Chaucer become reduced, with but few exceptions, to two contrasting forms:

dissh (*dish*)	*disshes* (*dish's*)
disshes (*dishes*)	*disshes* (*dishes'*)

It must be noticed that the ending spelled *–es* was pronounced with an *s,* not, as in modern English *dishes* (*dishez*), with a *z*. Nor was the termination conditioned, as it is in modern English, by the phonetic nature of the noun's final sound. Compare Chaucer's *disshes, cattes,* and *dogges* with the modern three-type system: *dishes* (*ez*), *cats* (*s*), and *dogs* (*z*).

Exceptions to the above declensional system are either still familiar, such as *goos* — *gees* (*goose* — *geese*) and *oxe* — *oxen* (*ox* — *oxen*), or are so rare that when they occur they can best be explained in the notes.

PRONOUNS

There are several important differences between Chaucer's pronouns and those used in modern English, as the following chart will show.

I	*thou*	*we*	*ye*
myn	*thyn*	*our*	*your*
me	*thee*	*us*	*you*

he	(*h*)*it*	*she*	*they*
his	*his*	*her*(*e*), *hir*(*e*)	*her*(*e*), *hir*(*e*)
him	*him* (dat.) (*h*)*it* (acc.)	*her*(*e*), *hir*(*e*)	*hem*

The only serious difficulty offered by the above set of pronouns lies in the fact that *her*(*e*) or *hir*(*e*) may mean, depending on context, either *her* or *their;* and *his* may, as in Shakespeare, mean either *his* or *its*.

ADJECTIVES

Chaucer still observed a distinction, now lost, between two different inflections of the adjective, the so-called strong and weak inflections, which were inherited from earlier English. The strong inflection of adjectives consists of a contrast between an absence of ending in the singular (*yong*) and the presence of a final *e* in the plural (*yonge*). It occurs after the indefinite article (*a* or *an*), or before an otherwise unmodified plural noun, or after a preposition, or as a predicate:

a *yong* knight	*yonge* knightes
of *yong* folk	of *yonge* knightes
he is *yong*	they been (are) *yonge*

The weak inflection, which has a final *e* in both the singular and the plural (*yonge*), occurs in all other situations:

the (this, myn) *yonge* knight	the (these, myne) *yonge* knightes
O *yonge knight*	O *yonge* knightes

With adjectives, such as *swete,* which have inherited a final *e* etymologically as part of their uninflected form, however, no such distinction can be made because the final *e* appears in all situations:

a *swete knight*	*swete* knightes
the *swete* knight	the *swete* knightes

VERBS

In Chaucer's English the past tense of verbs was formed in two basically different patterns, which still survive. Weak verbs (*love*) added a *d* or *t* to the stem; strong verbs (*drinke*) changed their stem vowel. The conjugational endings of the two classes differed, as they no longer do, only in the indicative singular of the past tense. The final *n* of the conjugational endings and the prefix *y–* of the past participle (here inserted in parenthesis) were beginning to disappear from the language. Chaucer used them or not at will.

Present Indicative

I *love*	*drinke*	we *love(n)*	*drinke(n)*
thou *lovest*	*drinkest*	ye *love(n)*	*drinke(n)*
he *loveth*	*drinketh*	they *love(n)*	*drinke(n)*

Subjunctive

I, thou, he *love*	*drinke*	we, ye they *love(n)*	*drinke(n)*

Past Indicative

I *lovede*	*drank*	we *lovede(n)*	*dronke(n)*
thou *lovedest*	*dronke*	ye *lovede(n)*	*dronke(n)*
he *lovede*	*drank*	they *lovede(n)*	*dronke(n)*

Subjunctive

I, thou, he *lovede*	*dronke*	we, ye, they *lovede(n)*	*dronke(n)*

Imperative

love *drink*(*e*) (thou) *loveth* *drinketh* (ye)

PAST PARTICIPLE	INFINITIVE
I have (*y–*)*loved* (*y–*)*dronke*(*n*)	to *love*(*n*) *drinke*(*n*)

Some verbs with stem ending in *d* or *t* regularly contracted the conjugational ending *–eth,* as in the following particularly common examples: he *bit* (biddeth), *fint* (findeth), *holt* (holdeth), *list* (listeth), *rit* (rideth), *stant* (standeth).

The only other irregularities of frequent occurrence likely to seem unfamiliar to the modern reader are the verb *to be,* which has the forms *we, ye, they be* or *been* in addition to the familiar *are*(n); and the following group of verbs which are peculiar both in form and meaning:

I *can,* thou *canst,* he *can;* we, ye, they *conne*(*n*) I *coude,* we *coude*(*n*) (conjugated like *lovede*)	(I can, know how)
I *may,* thou *mayst,* he *may;* we *mowe*(*n*) I *mighte*	(I can, am able)
I *moot,* thou *moost,* he *moot;* we *moote*(*n*) I *moste*	(I may, must)
I *woot,* thou *woost,* he *woot;* we *wite*(*n*) I *wiste*	(I know)

SYNTAX

Modern readers will find little in Chaucer's syntax that seems unfamiliar. Chaucer, like other poets before and since, in composing verse takes the liberty of inverting the word order normal to a prose sentence, but one of the chief characteristics of his style is its clarity. And when, on rare occasions, the logic of his sentence is irregular it merely matches the unconscious illogicalities of everyday speech.

VOCABULARY

Most of Chaucer's words, especially those of most frequent occurrence, have survived into modern English and have not notably changed in meaning. Some of his words have, however, become completely archaic, and their meanings must now be learned just as if they were words in a foreign language. And some apparently familiar words have subtly shifted in meaning since Chaucer's day and must therefore be reinterpreted.

The following literal translation of the opening lines of the *General Prologue* will exemplify the kind of problem in interpretation which faces the modern reader; and it can, at the same time, serve as an illustration of Chaucer's sentence construction.

Whan that Aprill with his shoures soote
The droghte of March hath perced to the roote
And bathed every veyne in swich licour
Of which vertu engendred is the flour,
Whan Zephirus eek with his sweete breeth
Inspired hath in every holt and heeth
The tendre croppes, and the yonge sonne
Hath in the Ram his half cours y-ronne,
And smale foweles maken melodye
That slepen al the nyght with open eye,
So priketh him Nature in hir corages,
Than longen folk to goon on pilgrymages,
And palmeres for to seken straunge strondes,
To ferne halwes kouthe in sondry londes.

(l. 1) When (*whan that* is more common than *whan* in Chaucer) April with its (the word *its* had not yet appeared in English) sweet showers has pierced the drought of March to the root and has bathed every vein in such liquid through the power of which the flower is engendered; (l. 5) when Zephyrus (the West Wind) also with its sweet breath has inspired (either in the etymological sense "breathed into," or "made to live," or both) the tender shoots in every wood and heath, and the young sun has run its half-course in the Ram (in the first stage of its annual journey through the signs of the zodiac), and small birds (not domestic *fowls* in the modern sense) make melody which sleep all the night with open eye — so much does Nature stir them in their hearts —; (l. 12) then people long to go on pilgrimages, and palmers (pilgrims who have carried back a palm leaf from Jerusalem) to seek unfamiliar shores, to distant shrines known in various lands.

The first sentence runs to a length and complexity quite unusual in Chaucer, but its structure, though loose, is effectively planned.

(1) *When* April has pierced . . . and bathed . . . ;

(5) *when* Zephyrus has inspired . . . ,

(7) and the sun has run . . . ,

(9) and birds make melody . . . (so much does Nature stir . . .);

(12) *then* people long to go . . . (and palmers [long] to seek . . .)
to distant shrines . . .

The problem of the meaning of words is obviously more serious than that of syntax. Only two words in the whole selection, *ferne* ("distant") and *halwes* ("shrines"), can be said to be extinct, and the latter is still familiar indirectly through the verb *to hallow* and the word *Halloween,* which means "Eve of All Hallows" ("hallowed persons" or saints). But several words such as *soote* ("sweet") do not immediately suggest their modern survivals because of extensive sound changes; and other words such as *licour* ("liquor"), because of subsequent extensions of meaning, are no longer familiar in the sense intended by Chaucer.

It is always difficult, moreover, to think within the frame of reference of a bygone age, yet we must attempt to if we wish to appreciate Chaucer's use of a word such as *corage* (l. 11). It is the ancestor of our word *courage* and can be roughly translated by the word "heart." But it suggested, for Chaucer's contemporaries, the animating spirit within the body which responds to the heart as the centre of feelings rather than to the brain as the centre of thought. It represents in medieval thought a counterpart to our current concept of the "autonomic nerve system," but only a partial counterpart. Chaucer's concept was in turn connected both with the theory of the four humours and with the belief in the influence of the planets, whereas our concept is allied with the theory of conditioned and unconditioned reflexes, and the like.

Chaucer himself was well aware of the relatively of language and of culture. "You know . . . that in form of speech there is change within a thousand years," he remarks in *Troilus and Criseyde,* "and that words that then had value now seem remarkably quaint and strange to us." "And yet," the people of the past "spoke them so and," he adds shrewdly, "succeeded as well . . . as men do now."

Ironically but inevitably, Chaucer's writing has suffered misunderstanding and neglect from posterity because of the apparent quaintness and strangeness of its language. In the seventeenth century, for instance, the brilliant poet and critic John Dryden, even though he admired and imitated Chaucer, failed to recognize Chaucer's metrical skill merely because he did not realize that his final *e*'s were to be pronounced. And, despite all the technical assistance afforded by modern scholarship, the reader of today must still make some adjustment if he is to enjoy the feeling that, when he reads Chaucer's poetry, he is reading the language once spoken by living men and women with minds and hearts like our own.

VERSIFICATION

Chaucer's copious repertoire of metres, hitherto unparalleled in English poetry, must have been inspired by his French and Italian contemporaries, whose techniques he probably learned not merely by close observation of their writings but also by personal conversations. The first known French treatise on the composition of vernacular rather than Latin poetry was written in 1392 by Eustache Deschamps, long after Chaucer had already displayed his own versatility; but the problems of versification must already have been discussed orally in France, just as they had been in Italy from the time of Dante, and we be sure that Chaucer, while travelling on the Continent, sought every opportunity for guidance on the subject.

In metre, rhyme and verse-form he shows a consistent skill which appears particularly striking when compared with that of his English contemporaries. In England two entirely different types of versification were currently popular, though the pious Parson repudiates both in the preamble to his tale. The one, representing a native tradition dating back before the Norman Conquest (1066), was based not upon rhyme or a fixed pattern of stressed syllables but upon alliteration. Surviving examples of its application contemporary with Chaucer are not numerous, although they include such poems as the brilliant anonymous romance *Sir Gawain and the Green Knight* and the widely read *Piers Plowman.* But the other type, which Chaucer adopted, was the familiar combination of rhyme and fixed stress-patterns which had gradually been adopted from the French after the Conquest and had become the dominant type of English versification.

The particular verse-form most commonly used in England during Chaucer's youth for purpose of narrative poetry was the four-beat couplet, and it was in this measure that Chaucer cast some of his earlier poetry, such as the *House of Fame*. But there is a danger that short lines with rhyme recurring every eight syllables will lapse into a tedious jog-trot, as indeed they did in the hands of lesser poets of the fourteenth century, and Chaucer with fine artistic sense departed from this limited verse-form early in his career. He became one of the first poets to introduce into English poetry the five beat line, and he experimented in it with a variety of rhyming combinations.

In the *Canterbury Tales,* among other metres, Chaucer used, apparently for the first time in English poetry, a five-beat, seven-line stanza, riming *ababbcc* (later known as the rhyme royal), for the *Man of Law's Tale,* the *Clerk's Tale,* the *Prioress's Tale,* and the *Second Nun's Tale.* A song in the *Clerk's Tale* is composed in five-beat, six-line stanzas rhyming *ababcb;* and the *Monk's Tale* is composed in five-beat, eight-line stanzas rhyming *ababbcbc.* Both of these metres were also new to English poetry. In *Sir Thopas* he used a medley of stanzaic forms. But the verse-form which he used most widely in the *Canterbury Tales* is the most famous, the five-beat couplet, later to be known as the heroic couplet.

Whatever verse form he uses, Chaucer gives the impression of being at ease. In one of his lyrics he complains of the scarcity of rhyming words in English as compared to French, but he rhymes accurately, hardly ever allowing himself to use a farfetched word or an imperfect rhyme. On occasions, it is true, he does use identical rhyme, as in the *General Prologue,* ll. 17-18:

> The holy, blisful martir for to *seke*
> That hem hath holpen whan that they were *seeke.*

But here, as elsewhere, the two rhyming words (one the ancestor of modern English *seek,* and the other of modern English *sick*) though identical in sound differ in origin and meaning. And he is certainly imitating the practice of French poets, who considered identical rhyme an adornment, not a fault.

Metrically, Chaucer is equally sure in his control of the underlying pattern which he has adopted, and here also he follows the practices of French poetry. He uses both masculine and feminine endings:

> Bifel that in that sesoun on a day
> In Southwerk at the Tabard, as I lay
> Redy to wenden on my pilgrymage
> To Caunterb(u)ry with ful devout corage.
> (*General Prologue,* ll. 19-22)

Here both lines of the first couplet end on a stressed tenth syllable (a masculine ending); both lines of the second couplet, on a stressed tenth syllable followed by an unstressed eleventh syllable (a feminine ending). He also varies at will the position of the stress within a metrical foot, as in *Redy to wenden.* Variations involving the insertion of extra syllables or the omission of syllables are perhaps often intended but may sometimes have resulted either from Chaucer's failure to revise his writing or from a scribe's careless recopying of a normal line.

As in French classical poetry, a final unstressed *e,* which in Chaucer's English was usually but not always pronounced, counted as one of the syllables of the metres, unless the *e* could be elided with a following word beginning either with a vowel or with an *h* followed by a vowel.

And which(e) they weren, and of what degree,
And eek in what array that they wer(e) inne.
(*General Prologue,* ll. 40-41)

Here the *e* of *whiche* was apparently not pronounced though written in most manuscripts. The final *e* of *were* (in the second line), which might have been pronounced, is here elided before a following vowel. In the first line, however, Chaucer uses the form *weren* instead of *were* and thereby avoids an unwanted elision with the vowel of *and,* availing himself, as he often does, of the optional variation in the conjugational ending *–e(n)*, which appears not merely, as here, in the past tense but also in the present, the infinitive, and the participle.

Chaucer usually allows each line to terminate some unit of a sentence, although less frequently than the next great master of the heroic couplet, John Dryden; but, like Dryden, he attains freedom within the line by skillful variation in his use of the sentence pause or caesura. The rapid phrasing of the comic lines describing a widow's pursuit of a fox who has stolen her rooster may be compared, for instance, with the tragic lines describing a widow's vain search for her missing son:

The sely widw(e) and eek hir(e) doghtres two
Herden this(e) hennes cry(e) and maken wo,
And out att(e) dores stirten they anon.
(*Nun's Priest's Tale,* ll. 555-57)

This poure wydw(e) awaiteth al that nyght
After hir litel child, || but he cam noght.
(*Prioress's Tale,* ll. 134-35)

Chaucer's versification is in itself masterly, but it derives its effectiveness from his larger mastery of poetic creativity. A superficial reading of Chaucer's poetry may suggest simplicity, but the sensitive reader soon comes to realize that Chaucer has cunningly concealed the pains bestowed upon his art. We might, in fact, apply to it the words which in the *Parliament of Birds* he applies to the art of love: "The life so short, the craft so long to learn! The attempt so hard, so keen the victory!"

THE

PROLOGUE

TO THE

CANTERBURY

TALES

HERE BEGINS THE BOOK OF THE TALES OF CANTERBURY

When April with his showers sweet
The drought of March has pierced to the root,
And bathed every vein in such liquor,
Of whose virtue is engendered the flower;
When Zephyr too with his sweet breath
Has made alive in every grove and field
The tender sprouts, and the young sun
Has in the Ram his half course run,
And small birds make melody
That sleep all night with open eye—
So Nature goads them in their hearts—
Then people long to go on pilgrimages,
And palmers to seek strange shores
To far-off shrines, known in various lands;
And specially from every shires' end
Of England, to Canterbury they wend,
The holy blessed martyr to seek
Who helped them when they were sick.
It happened that, in that season on a day,
In Southwark, at the Tabard as I lay,
Ready to travel on my pilgrimage
To Canterbury with a fully devout heart,
At night there came into that inn
Full nine and twenty in a company
Of sundry folk, by chance fallen
Into fellowship, and pilgrims were they all
That toward Canterbury would ride.
The chambers and the stables were large,
And well were we treated with the best.
In brief, when the sun had gone to rest,
I had so spoken with them, every one,
That I was forthwith of their fellowship,
And made an agreement to rise early
And take our way, as I shall tell you.
But nevertheless, while I have time and space,
Before I further in this tale proceed,
I think it reasonable
To tell you all about the nature
Of each of them, as they appeared to me,
And who they were, and of what rank,

HERE BYGYNNETH THE BOOK OF THE TALES OF CANTERBURY

Whan that Aprill with his shoures soote
The droghte of March hath perced to the roote,
And bathed every veyne in swich licour,
Of which vertu engendred is the flour;
Whan Zephyrus eek with his sweete breeth
Inspired hath in every holt and heeth
The tendre croppes, and the yonge sonne
Hath in the Ram his halfe cours yronne,
And smale foweles maken melodye
That slepen al the nyght with open yë—
So priketh hem Nature in hir corages—
Thanne Longen folk to goon on pilgrimages,
And palmeres for to seken straunge strondes
To ferne halwes, kouthe in sondry londes;
And specially from every shires ende
Of Engelond to Caunterbury they wende,
The holy blisful martir for to seke
That hem hath holpen whan that they were seeke.
Bifel that in that seson on a day,
In Southwerk at the Tabard as I lay,
Redy to wenden on my pilgrymage
To Caunterbury with ful devout corage,
At nyght was come into that hostelrye
Wel nyne and twenty in a compaignye
Of sondry folk, by aventure yfalle
In felaweshipe, and pilgrimes were they alle
That toward Caunterbury wolden ryde.
The chambres and the stables weren wyde,
And wel we weren esed atte beste.
And shortly, whan the sonne was to reste,
So hadde I spoken with hem everichon
That I was of hir felaweshipe anon,
And made forward erly for to ryse
To take oure way ther-as I yow devyse.
But nathelees, whil I have tyme and space,
Er that I ferther in this tale pace,
Me thynketh it acordaunt to resoun
To telle yow al the condicioun
Of ech of hem, so as it seemed me,
And whiche they weren, and of what degree,

And also in what clothes they were dressed;
And with a knight then will I first begin.
A Knight there was, and he a worthy man,
That from the time that he first began
To ride forth, he loved chivalry,
Truth and honour, generosity and courtesy.
Full worthy was he in his lord's war,
And in these he had ridden (no man farther),
In both Christian and in heathen lands,
And was ever honoured for his worthiness.
At Alexandria he was, when it was won.
Many a time he had headed the table
Over those of all nations, in Prussia;
In Lithuania he had fought, and in Russia,
More than any other Christian of his rank.
In Grenada, too, he had been at the siege
Of Algeciras, and ridden in Benmarin.
At Ayas was he, and at Adalia
When they were won; and in the Great Sea
With many a noble expedition had he been.
In fifteen mortal battles he had engaged,
And fought for our faith at Tlemcen
Three times in the lists, and always slain his foe.
This same worthy knight had also been
Once with the lord of Palatia
Against another heathen in Turkey.
And evermore he had a noble reputation;
And even though he was valiant, he was wise,
And in his manner as modest as a maiden.
He had never uttered any vileness
In all his life to any kind of person.
He was a truly perfect gentle knight.
But to tell you of his dress,
His horses were good, but he was not gaudy.
Of coarse cloth he wore a doublet
All stained by his coat of mail,
For he had lately come from a voyage,
And went to make his pilgrimage.
With him was his son, a young Squire,
A lover, and a lusty aspirant for knighthood,
With locks curled, as though from a curling-iron.
About twenty years old he was, I guess.
In stature he was of average height,
And wonderfully agile, and of great strength.

And eek in what array that they were inne;
And at a knyght than wol I first bigynne.
 A Knyght ther was, and that a worthy man,
That fro the tyme that he first bigan
To riden out, he loved chivalrye,
Trouthe and honour, fredom and curteisye.
Full worthy was he in his lordes werre,
And therto hadde he riden, no man ferre,
As wel in Cristendom as in hethenesse,
And evere honoured for his worthynesse.
At Alisaundre he was whan it was wonne.
Ful ofte tyme he hadde the bord bigonne
Aboven alle nacions in Pruce;
In Lettow had he reysed, and in Ruce,
No Cristen man so ofte of his degree.
In Gernade at the seege eek hadde he be
Of Algezir, and riden in Belmarye.
At Lyeys was he, and at Satalye
Whan they were wonne; and in the Grete See
At many a noble armee hadde he be.
At mortal batailles hadde he been fiftene,
And foughten for oure feith at Tramyssene
In lystes thries, and ay slayn his foo.
 This ilke worthy knyght hadde been also
Somtyme with the lord of Palatye
Agayn another hethen in Turkye.
And everemoore he hadde a sovereyn prys;
And though that he were worthy, he was wys,
And of his port as meeke as is a mayde.
He nevere yet no vileynye ne sayde
In al his lyf unto no maner wight.
He was a verray, parfit, gentil knyght.
But for to tellen yow of his array,
His hors were goode, but he was nat gay.
Of fustian he wered a gypon
Al bismotered with his habergeon,
For he was late ycome from his viage
And wente for to doon his pilgrymage.
 With him ther was his sone, a yong Squier,
A lovere and a lusty bacheler,
With lokkes crulle as they were leyd in presse.
Of twenty yeer of age he was, I gesse.
Of his stature he was of evene lengthe,
And wonderly delyvere, and of great strengthe.

And he had been once in the cavalry,
In Flanders, in Artois and Picardy,
And bore himself well, considering his short service,
In hope of standing in his lady's grace.
Embroidered was he like a meadow,
All full of fresh flowers, white and red.
Singing he was, or fluting, all the day;
He was as fresh as is the month of May.
Short was his gown, with sleeves long and wide.
Well could he sit his horse, and fairly ride;
He could make songs and compose well,
Joust and also dance, and draw and write well.
He loved so hotly that at night-time
He slept no more than does a nightingale.
Courteous he was, humble, and serviceable,
And carved before his father at the table.
  A Yeoman had he, and no other servants
At that time, for he preferred to travel so,
And he was clad in coat and hood of green.
A sheaf of peacock arrows, bright and sharp,
Under his belt he bore right carefully;
Well could he handle his equipment yeomanly:
His arrows didn't droop with trailing feathers.
And in his hand he bore a mighty bow
A cropped head had he and a brown face.
Woodcraft he understood thoroughly.
Upon his arm he bore a gay arm-guard,
And by his side a sword and buckler,
And on the other side a fine dagger,
Mounted well and sharp as a spear-point;
A silver Christopher shone upon his breast.
A horn he bore, the carrying-strap was green;
He was truly a forester, as I guess.
  There was also a Nun, a Prioress,
That in her smiling was simple and sweet.
Her greatest oath was but 'by Saint Loy';
And she was called Madame Eglentine.
Full well she sang the divine service,
Intoned in her nose full seemly;
And she spoke French fluently and elegantly,
According to the school of Stratford-at-Bow,
For Parisian French was unknown to her.
At meals well taught was she withal:
She let no morsel from her lips fall,

And he hadde been som tyme in chivachye
In Flaundres, in Artoys, and Picardye,
And born him wel as of so litel space,
In hope to stonden in his lady grace.
Embrouded was he as it were a meede,
Al ful of fresshe floures whyte and reede.
Syngynge he was, or floytynge, al the day;
He was as fressh as is the month of May.
Short was his gowne, with sleves longe and wyde.
Wel koude he sitte on hors and faire ryde;
He koude songes make and wel endite,
Juste and eek daunce, and wel purtreye and write.
So hote he lovede that by nyghtertale
He slepte namoore than dooth a nyghtyngale.
Curteis he was, lowely, and servysable,
And carf biforn his fader at the table.
  A Yeman hadde he and servantz namo
At that tyme, for hym liste ride so,
And he was clad in cote and hood of grene.
A sheef of pecok arwes, bright and kene,
Under his belt he bar ful thriftily;
Wel koude he dresse his takel yemanly:
His arwes drouped noght with fetheres lowe.
And in his hand he bar a myghty bowe.
A not heed hadde he with a broun visage.
Of wodecraft wel koude he al the usage.
Upon his arm he bar a gay bracer,
And by his syde a swerd and a bokeler,
And on that oother syde a gay daggere,
Harneised wel and sharpe as point of spere;
A Cristophre on his brest of silver sheene.
An horn he bar, the bawdryk was of grene;
A forster was he soothly, as I gesse.
  Ther was also a Nonne, a Prioresse,
That of hir smylyng was ful symple and coy.
Hir gretteste ooth was but by Seint Loy;
And she was cleped Madame Eglentyne.
Ful wel she soong the service dyvyne,
Entuned in hir nose ful semely;
And Frenssh she spak ful faire and fetisly,
After the scole of Stratford atte Bowe,
For Frenssh of Parys was to hire unknowe.
At mete wel ytaught was she with alle:
She leet no morsel from hir lippes falle,

Nor wet her fingers deeply in her sauce;
Well could she handle a morsel, and be careful
That no drop ever fell upon her breast.
Courtesy was her particular interest.
Her upper lip she wiped so clean
That in her cup was no trace seen
Of grease, when she had drunk her draught;
Politely after her food she reached.
And certainly she was very cheerful,
And very pleasant, and amiable of disposition,
And she took pains to simulate the behaviour
Of court, and be stately in manner,
And to be held worthy of reverence.
But, to speak of her inner nature,
She was so charitable and full of pity
That she would weep if she saw a mouse
Caught in a trap, if it were dead or bleeding.
Some small dogs had she that she fed
With roasted meat, or milk and finest bread;
But sorely would she weep if one of them were dead,
Or if men struck it smartly with a stick;
And she was all feeling and tender-heartedness.
Most neatly her wimple was pleated,
Her nose well-shaped, her eyes grey as glass,
Her mouth very small, and also soft and red;
But certainly she had a fair forehead;
It was almost a span broad, I believe,
For certainly, she was not undersized.
Her cloak was very neat, I was aware;
Of small coral about her arm she bore
A rosary, the larger beads of green,
And thereon hung a brooch of brightest gold,
On which there was first written a crowned A,
And after *Amor vincit omnia.*

Another Nun with her had she,
Who was her chaplain, and three priests.

A Monk there was, a masterful person,
An outrider that loved hunting,
A manly man, capable of being an abbot.
Full many a valuable horse had he in stable,
And when he rode, men might his bridle hear
Jingling in a whistling wind as clear
And also as loud as the chapel bell.
There where this lord was head of the cell,

Ne wette hir fyngres in hir sauce depe;
Wel koude she carie a morsel, and wel kepe
That no drope ne fille upon hir brest.
In curteisie was set ful muchel hir lest.
Hir over-lippe wyped she so clene
That in hir coppe ther was no ferthyng sene
Of grece, when she dronken hadde hir draughte;
Ful semely after hir mete she raughte.
And sikerly she was of greet desport,
And ful plesaunt, and amyable of port,
And peyned hire to countrefete cheere
Of court, and to been estatlich of manere,
And to been holden digne of reverence.
But for to speken of hir conscience,
She was so charitable and so pitous
She wolde wepe if that she sawe a mous
Caught in a trappe, if it were deed or bledde.
Of smale houndes hadde she that she fedde
With rosted flessh, or milk and wastel-breed;
But soore wepte she if oon of hem were deed,
Or if men smoot it with a yerde smerte;
And al was conscience and tendre herte.
Ful semely hir wympel pynched was,
Hir nose tretys, hir eyen greye as glas,
Hir mouth ful smal, and therto softe and reed;
But sikerly she hadde a fair forheed;
It was almoost a spanne brood, I trowe,
For hardily, she was nat undergrowe.
Ful fetys was hir cloke, as I was war;
Of smal coral aboute hir arm she bar
A peire of bedes, gauded al with grene,
And theron heng a brooch of gold ful sheene,
On which ther was first write a crowned A,
And after *Amor vincit omnia.*
  Another Nonne with hire hadde she,
That was hire chapeleyne and preestes thre.
  A Monk ther was, a fair for the maistrie,
An outridere that lovede venerye,
A manly man, to been an abbot able.
Ful many a deyntee hors hadde he in stable,
And whan he rood, men myghte his brydel heere
Gynglen in a whistlynge wynd as cleere
And eek as loude as dooth the chapel belle.
Ther as this lord was kepere of the celle,

The rule of Saint Maur or of Saint Benedict,
Because it was old and somewhat strict,
This same monk let such old things pass,
And followed the customs of the new world meanwhile.
He did not give a plucked hen for that text
That says that hunters are not holy men,
Nor that a monk, when he is neglectful of rule,
Is like a fish without water—
That is to say, a monk without a cloister.
But this text he held not worth an oyster;
And I said his opinion was good.
Why should he study and drive himself mad,
Always poring over a book in the cloister,
Or work with his hands, and labour,
As St. Augustine bids? How shall the world be served?
Let St. Augustine have his work reserved for himself!
Therefore he was a true huntsman.
He had greyhounds as swift as birds in flight;
In tracking and hunting for the hare
Was all his pleasure, for no cost would he spare.
I saw his sleeves trimmed at the hand
With grey fur, and that the finest in the land;
And to fasten his hood under his chin,
He had of wrought gold an intricate pin;
A love-knot in the large end there was.
His head was bald, and shone like glass,
And also his face, as if he had been anointed;
He was a lord, fat and in good condition.
His eyes sharp, and rolling in his head,
That glowed like a fire under a cauldron,
His boots supple, his horse in fine shape,
Now certainly he was a fair prelate.
He was not pale like a tormented ghost;
A fat swan loved he best of any roast.
His palfrey was as brown as a berry.

A Friar there was, a wanton and a merry one,
A limiter, a very festive man.
In all the four orders there is no one that knows
So much of gossip and flattering language.
He had performed many a marriage
Of young women at his own cost.
He was a noble pillar of his order.
Well loved and familiar was he
With rich farmers over all his country,

The reule of Seint Maure or of Seint Beneit,
By cause that it was old and somdel streit,
This ilke Monk leet olde thynges pace,
And heeld after the newe world the space.
He yaf nat of that text a pulled hen
That seith that hunters been nat holy men,
Ne that a monk, whan he is recchelees,
Is likned til a fissh that is waterlees—
This is to seyn, a monk out of his cloystre.
But thilke text heeld he nat worth an oystre;
And I seyde his opinion was good.
What sholde he studie and make hymselven wood,
Upon a book in cloystre alwey to poure,
Or swynken with his handes and laboure,
As Austyn bit? How shal the world be served?
Lat Austyn have his swynk to him reserved!
Therfore he was a prikasour aright.
Grehoundes he hadde as swift as fowel in flight;
Of prikyng and of huntyng for the hare
Was al his lust, for no cost wolde he spare.
I seigh his sleves purfiled at the hond
With grys, and that the fyneste of a lond;
And for to festne his hood under his chyn,
He hadde of gold yroght a ful curious pyn;
A love-knotte in the gretter ende ther was.
His heed was balled, that shoon as any glas,
And eek his face, as he hadde been enoynt;
He was a lord ful fat and in good poynt.
His eyen stepe, and rollynge in his heed,
That stemed as a forneys of a leed,
His bootes souple, his hors in greet estaat,
Now certeinly he was a fair prelaat.
He was nat pale as a forpyned goost;
A fat swan loved he best of any roost.
His palfrey was as broun as is a berye.
    A Frere ther was, a wantowne and a merye,
A lymytour, a ful solempne man.
In alle the ordres foure is noon that kan
So muche of daliaunce and fair langage.
He hadde maad ful many a mariage
Of yonge wommen at his owene cost.
Unto his ordre he was a noble post.
Ful wel biloved and famulier was he
With frankeleyns over al in his contree,

And also with worthy women of the town;
For he was empowered to hear confession,
As he said himself, more than a parish priest,
For in his order he held a papal licence.
Most sweetly heard he confession,
And pleasant was his absolution.
He was an easy man in giving penance
When he knew he would have a good remuneration;
For to give to a poor order
Is a sign that a man is well shriven;
For if one gave, he dared assert
He knew that man was repentant;
For many a man is so hard of heart,
He cannot weep even though he suffers sorely.
Therefore, instead of weeping and prayers,
Men should give silver to the poor friars.
His hood was always stuffed with knives
And pins, to give to fair women.
And certainly he had a merry note;
He could sing well and play on the fiddle;
In songs he easily took the prize.
His neck was white as the lily;
Yet he was as strong as a champion.
He knew the taverns well in every town,
And every innkeeper and barmaid,
Better than he did a leper or a female beggar.
For such a worthy man as he
It was not fitting, considering his position,
To be acquainted with sick lepers.
It is not worthy, it holds no profit,
To deal with such poor people,
But rather with the rich, and the sellers of food.
And anywhere, wherever profit might appear,
He was courteous, and humble in his service;
There was no man anywhere so virtuous.
He was the best beggar in his house,
For though a widow had not even a shoe,
So pleasant was his *In principio*
That he would have a farthing ere he left.
His collections were larger than his income.
And he could play as though he were a puppy;
On love-days he was a great help,
For there he was not like a cloisterer
With threadbare cape, as is a poor scholar,

And eek with worthy wommen of the toun;
For he hadde power of confessioun,
As seyde hymself, moore than a curat,
For of his ordre he was licenciat.
Ful swetely herde he confession,
And plesaunt was his absolucion.
He was an esy man to yeve penaunce
Ther as he wiste to have a good pitaunce;
For unto a povre ordre for to yive
Is signe that a man is wel yshryve;
For if he yaf, he dorste make avaunt
He wiste that a man was repentaunt;
For many a man so hard is of his herte,
He may nat wepe althogh hym soore smerte.
Therfore, instede of wepynge and prayeres,
Men moote yeve silver to the povre freres.
His typet was ay farsed ful of knyves
And pynnes, for to yeven faire wyves.
And certeinly he hadde a murye note;
Wel koude he synge and pleyen on a rote;
Of yeddynges he baar outrely the pris.
His nekke whit was as the flour-de-lys;
Therto he strong was as a champioun.
He knew the tavernes wel in every toun,
And every hostiler and tappestere,
Bet than a lazar or a beggestere.
For unto swich a worthy man as he
Acorded nat, as by his facultee,
To have with sike lazars aqueyntaunce.
It is nat honeste, it may nat avaunce,
For to deelen with no swich poraille,
But al with riche, and selleres of vitaille.
And over al ther as profit sholde arise,
Curteis he was, and lowely of servyse;
Ther nas no man nowher so vertuous.
He was the beste beggere in his hous,
For thogh a wydwe hadde noght a sho,
So plesaunt was his *In principio*
Yet wolde he have a ferthyng er he wente.
His purchas was wel bettre than his rente.
And rage he koude as it were right a whelpe;
In love-dayes ther koude he muchel helpe,
For ther he was nat lyk a cloysterer
With a thredbare cope, as is a povre scoler,

But he was like a high official or a pope.
Of double-worsted was his half-cape,
And rounded as the mold of a bell.
He lisped a little as an affectation,
To make his English sweet upon the tongue;
And in his harping, when he had sung,
His eyes twinkled in his head aright
As do the stars in the frosty night.
This worthy limiter was called Hubert.
A Merchant was there with a forked beard,
In motley, and high on his horse he sat;
Upon his head a Flemish beaver hat,
His boots fastened neatly and elegantly.
His opinions he spoke most solemnly,
Proclaiming always the increase of his profits.
He wanted the sea guarded at any price
Between Middleburg and Orwell.
Well could he in bargaining sell French crowns.
This worthy man kept all his wits about him:
No one knew that he was in debt,
So dignified was he in his dealings,
With his bargainings, and with his borrowings.
For truly he was a worthy man withal,
But truth to tell, I do not know what he was called.
A Clerk there was of Oxford also,
Who to logic had long given himself.
As lean was his horse as is a rake,
And he was not exactly fat, I might add,
But looked hollow-cheeked, and likewise sober.
Quite threadbare was his outer cloak,
For he had not yet gotten himself a benefice,
Nor was worldly enough to seek office.
For he would rather have at his bed's head
Twenty books, bound in black and red,
Of Aristotle and his philosophy,
Than rich robes, or a fiddle, or a gay harp.
But although he was a philosopher,
Yet had he little gold in his coffer;
But all that he might get from his friends,
On books and learning he spent,
And busily prayed for the souls
Of those that gave him wherewithal to study.
Of study took he most care and most heed.
Not a word did he speak more than was needed,

But he was lyk a maister or a pope.
Of double worstede was his semycope,
And rounded as a belle out of the presse.
Somwhat he lipsed for his wantownesse,
To make his Englissh sweete upon his tonge;
And in his harpyng, whan that he hadde songe,
His eyen twynkled in his heed aryght
As doon the sterres in the frosty nyght.
This worthy lymytour was cleped Huberd.
  A Marchant was ther with a forked berd,
In mottelee, and hye on horse he sat;
Upon his heed a Flaundryssh bevere hat,
His bootes clasped faire and fetisly.
His resons he spak ful solempnely,
Sownynge alway th'encrees of his wynnyng.
He wolde the see were kept for any thing
Betwixen Middelburgh and Orewelle.
Wel koude he in eschaunge sheeldes selle.
This worthy man ful wel his wit besette:
Ther wiste no wight that he was in dette,
So estatly was he of his governaunce,
With his bargaynes, and with his chevyssaunce.
For sothe he was a worthy man with alle,
But, sooth to seyn, I noot how men hym calle.
  A Clerk ther was of Oxenford also,
That unto logyk hadde longe ygo.
As leene was his hors as is a rake,
And he nas nat right fat, I undertake,
But looked holwe, and therto sobrely.
Ful thredbare was his overeste courtepy,
For he hadde geten hym yet no benefice,
Ne was so worldly for to have office.
For hym was levere have at his beddes heed
Twenty bookes, clad in blak or reed,
Of Aristotle and his philosophie,
Than robes riche, or fithele, or gay sautrie.
But al be that he was a philosophre,
Yet hadde he but litel gold in cofre;
But al that he myghte of his freendes hente,
On bookes and on lernynge he it spente,
And bisily gan for the soules preye
Of hem that yaf him wherwith to scoleye.
Of studie took he moost cure and moost heede.
Noght o word spak he moore than was neede,

And that was said with propriety and modesty,
And brief and lively, and full of high meaning;
Concerned with moral virtue was his speech,
And gladly would he learn and gladly teach.
A Sergeant-of-Law, wary and wise,
Who often had been at the church porch,
There was also, rich in excellence.
Discreet he was, and of great reverence—
He seemed so, his words were so wise.
A justice was he often in assize,
By patent and by full commission.
For his knowledge and for his high renown
Of fees and robes had he many a one.
So great a buyer of land was nowhere known;
All was fee simple to him in effect;
His purchases could not be contested.
There was nowhere so busy a man as he,
And yet he seemed busier than he was.
He could recite all the cases and judgements,
That had taken place from the time of King William.
He could so draw up and make a document,
That no man could find a flaw in his writing;
And every statute he could recite by rote.
He rode unpretentiously in a motley coat,
Belted with a girdle of silk with small stripes.
Of his dress I tell no longer tale.
A Franklin was in his company;
White was his beard as is the daisy;
Of a ruddy complexion.
Well loved he in the morning a sop of wine;
To live pleasurably was ever his custom,
For he was Epicurus' own son,
Who held the theory that complete delight
Was truly the perfect felicity.
A householder, and a great one, was he;
Saint Julian he was in his country.
His bread, his ale were always equally good;
A man with a better wine-cellar did not exist.
His house was never without meat pie,
Of fish and flesh, and that so plenteous,
It snowed in his house of meat and drink,
Of all dainties that one could think of.
According to the various seasons of the year,
He varied his meat and his supper.

And that was seyd in forme and reverence,
And short and quyk, and ful of hy sentence;
Sownynge in moral vertu was his speche,
And gladly wolde he lerne and gladly teche.
A Sergeant of the Lawe, war and wys,
That often hadde been at the Parvys,
Ther was also, ful riche of excellence.
Discreet he was, and of greet reverence—
He seemed swich, his wordes weren so wise.
Justice he was ful often in assise,
By patente and by pleyn commissioun.
For his science and for his heigh renoun
Of fees and robes hadde he many oon.
So greet a purchasour was nowher noon;
Al was fee symple to hym in effect;
His purchasyng myghte nat been infect.
Nowher so bisy a man as he ther nas,
And yet he semed bisier than he was.
In termes hadde he caas and doomes alle
That from the tyme of kyng William were falle.
Therto he koude endite and make a thyng,
Ther koude no wight pynche at his writyng;
And every statut koude he pleyn by rote.
He rood but hoomly in a medlee cote,
Girt with a ceint of silk with barres smale.
Of his array telle I no lenger tale.
A Frankeleyn was in his compaignye;
Whit was his berd as is the dayesye;
Of his complexion he was sangwyn.
Wel loved he by the morwe a sop in wyn;
To lyven in delit was evere his wone,
For he was Epicurus owene sone,
That heeld opinion that pleyn delit
Was verraily felicitee parfit.
An housholdere, and that a greet, was he;
Saint Julian he was in his contree.
His breed, his ale, was alweys after oon;
A bettre envyned man was nowher noon.
Withoute bake mete was nevere his hous,
Of fissh and flessh, and that so plentevous,
It snewed in his hous of mete and drynke,
Of alle deyntees that men koude thynke.
After the sondry sesons of the yeer,
So chaunged he his mete and his soper.

Full many a fat partridge had he in coop,
And many a bream and many a pike in his pond.
Woe to his cook, unless his sauce were
Pungent and sharp, and all his equipment ready.
His table stationed in his hall always
Stood ready set all the day long.
At court sessions was he lord and sire;
Often he was knight of the shire.
A dagger and a pouch of silk
Hung at his girdle, white as morning milk.
A sheriff had he been, and a treasurer.
There was nowhere such a worthy vassal.
  A Haberdasher and a Carpenter,
A Weaver, a Dyer, and an Upholsterer—
Were with us too, clothed in one livery
Of a distinguished and great guild.
Full fresh and new their clothes were trimmed;
Their knives were mounted not with brass,
But all with silver; wrought full clean and well
Their girdles and their pouches were in keeping.
Each of them seemed a sufficiently good citizen
To sit in a guildhall on a dais.
Each, for the knowledge that he had,
Was fit to be an alderman.
For property had they enough and income,
And also their wives would agree to it—
And otherwise certainly they would be to blame.
It is indeed pleasant to be called "Madam",
And go to vigils before everyone,
And have a mantle royally carried.
  A Cook they had with them for the occasion,
To boil the chickens with the marrow bones,
And tart flavouring and spice.
Well could he appreciate a draught of London ale.
He could roast and boil and fry,
Make a stew, and well bake a pie.
But a great pity was it, as I thought,
That on his shin he had an ulcer,
As for spiced chicken, he made that with the best.
  A Sailor was there, living to the west;
For all I know, he was from Dartmouth.
He rode upon a large horse as well as he could,
In a gown of coarse cloth to the knee.
A dagger hanging on a cord had he

Ful many a fat partrich hadde he in muwe,
And many a breem and many a luce in stuwe.
Wo was his cook but if his sauce were
Poynaunt and sharp, and redy al his geere.
His table dormant in his halle alway
Stood redy covered al the longe day.
At sessions ther was he lord and sire;
Ful ofte tyme he was knyght of the shire.
An anlaas and a gipser al of silk
Heeng at his girdel, whit as morne milk.
A shirreve hadde he been, and a countour.
Was nowher swich a worthy vasasour.
An Haberdasshere and a Carpenter,
A Webbe, a Dyere, and a Tapycer—
And they were clothed alle in o lyveree
Of a solempne and a greet fraternitee.
Ful fressh and newe hir geere apiked was;
Hir knyves were chaped noght with bras,
But al with silver; wroght ful clene and weel
Hire girdles and hir pouches everydeel.
Wel seemed ech of hem a fair burgeys
To sitten in a yeldehalle on a deys.
Everich, for the wisdom that he kan,
Was shaply for to been an alderman.
For catel hadde they ynogh and rente,
And eek hir wyves wolde it wel assente—
And elles certeyn were they to blame.
It is ful fair to been ycleped "Madame,"
And goon to vigilies al bifore,
And have a mantel roialliche ybore.
A Cook they hadde with hem for the nones.
To boille the chiknes with the marybones,
And powdre-marchant tart and galyngale.
Wel koude he knowe a draughte of London ale.
He koude rooste and sethe and broille and frye,
Maken mortreux, and wel bake a pye.
But greet harm was it, as it thoughte me,
That on his shyne a mormal hadde he.
For blankmanger, that mare he with the beste.
A Shipman was ther, wonynge fer by weste;
For aught I woot, he was of Dertemouthe.
He rood upon a rouncy as he kouthe,
In a gowne of faldyng to the knee.
A daggere hangynge on a laas hadde he

Around his neck and beneath his arm.
The hot summer had made his colour brown;
And certainly he was a good fellow.
Full many a draught of wine had he drawn
Coming from Bordeaux, while the merchant slept;
Of scrupulous conscience he took no heed.
If he fought and gained the upper hand,
By water he sent them home to every land.
But as to his skill in reckoning his tides,
His currents and his other dangers besides,
His harbour and his moon, his pilotage,
There was none such from Hull to Carthage.
Hardy he was and shrewd in his ventures;
By many a tempest had his beard been shaken;
He knew all the harbours as they were,
From Gotland to the Cape of Finisterre,
And every creek in Brittany and Spain.
His ship was called the Madelaine.
 With us there was a Doctor of Medicine;
In all this world there never was his like,
To speak of medicine and surgery,
For he was grounded in astrology.
He cared for his patient very carefully
According to the stars, by his natural magic.
Well could he understand the fortunes of the rise
Of the signs pertaining to his patient.
He knew the cause of every sickness,
Whether of hot or cold or moist or dry,
And where engendered and of which humour;
He was a very perfect practicioner.
The cause known, and of his disease the root,
At once he gave the sick man his remedy.
All ready had he his apothecaries
To send him his drugs and medicines,
For each of them made profit for the other;
Their friendship had not just begun.
Well did he know the old Aesculapias,
And Dioscorides, and also Rufus,
Old Hippocrates, Haly and Galen,
Serapion, Rhasis, and Avicenna,
Averroes, Damascene, and Constantine,
Bernard and Gatisden and Gilbertine.
In his diet he was moderate,
For it had no superfluity,

Aboute his nekke, under his arm adoun.
The hoote somer hadde maad his hewe al broun;
And certeinly he was a good felawe.
Ful many a draughte of wyn hadde he ydrawe
Fro Burdeux-ward, whil that the chapman sleep;
Of nyce conscience took he no keep.
If that he faught and hadde the hyer hond,
By water he sente hem hoom to every lond.
But of his craft, to rekene wel his tydes,
His stremes and his daungers hym bisides,
His herberwe and his moone, his lodemenage,
Ther nas noon swich from Hulle to Cartage.
Hardy he was and wys to undertake;
With many a tempest hadde his berd been shake;
He knew alle the havenes as they were,
Fro Gootlond to the Cape of Fynystere,
And every cryke in Britaigne and in Spayne.
His barge ycleped was the Maudelayne.
With us ther was a Doctour of Phisik;
In al this world ne was ther noon hym lik,
To speke of phisik and of surgerye,
For he was grounded in astronomye.
He kepte his pacient a ful greet deel
In houres by his magyk natureel.
Wel koude he fortunen the ascendent
Of his ymages for his pacient.
He knew the cause of every maladye,
Were it of hoot or cold or moyste or drye,
And where engendred and of what humour;
He was a verray, parfit praktisour.
The cause yknowe, and of his harm the roote,
Anon he yaf the sike man his boote.
Ful redy hadde he his apothecaries
To sende him drogges and his letuaries,
For ech of hem made oother for to wynne;
Hir frendshipe nas nat newe to bigynne.
Wel knew he the olde Esculapius,
And Deiscorides and eek Rufus,
Olde Ypocras, Haly, and Galyen,
Serapion, Razis, and Avycen,
Averrois, Damascien, and Constantyn,
Bernard and Gatesden and Gilbertyn.
Of his diete mesurable was he,
For it was of no superfluitee,

But was greatly nourishing and digestible.
His study was but little of the Bible.
In blood-red and blue-gray he was clad,
Lined with taffeta and fine silk;
And yet he was slow in spending;
He kept what he earned during the plague;
For gold in medicine is a cordial,
Therefore he loved gold especially.
A good Wife was there from near Bath,
But she was somewhat deaf, and that was a pity.
Of cloth-making she had such a knack,
She surpased them of Ypres and Ghent.
In all the parish woman was there none
That to the collection box before her should go;
And if any did, certainly so angry was she,
That she lost all charity.
Her kerchiefs were finely woven;
I dare swear they weighed ten pounds
That on a Sunday were upon her head.
Her hose were of fine scarlet red,
Tightly tied, and shoes all soft and new.
Bold was her face, and fair, and red of hue.
She was a worthy woman all her life:
Husbands at church door she had five,
Not to mention other companions in youth—
But there is no need to discuss that now.
And thrice had she been at Jerusalem;
She had crossed many a foreign stream;
At Rome she had been, and at Boulogne,
In Galicia at Saint James, and at Cologne;
She knew much of wayfaring.
Gap-toothed was she, to tell the truth.
Upon an ambling horse easily she sat,
Neatly veiled, and on her head a hat
As wide as a buckler or a shield;
An outer skirt about her large hips,
And on her feet a pair of sharp spurs.
In company well could she laugh and joke.
She doubtless knew the remedies of love,
For she knew that art from of old.
A good man there was of religion,
Who was a poor Parson of a town,
But he was rich in holy thought and work.
He was also a learned man, a clerk,

But of greet norissyng and digestible.
His studie was but litel on the Bible.
In sangwyn and in pers he clad was al,
Lyned with taffata and with sendal;
And yet he was but esy of dispence;
He kepte that he wan in pestilence.
For gold in phisik is a cordial,
Therfore he loved gold in special.
A good Wif was ther of biside Bathe,
But she was somdel deef, and that was scathe.
Of clooth-makyng she hadde swich an haunt,
She passed hem of Ypres and of Gaunt.
In al the parisshe wif ne was ther noon
That to the offrynge bifore hire sholde goon;
And if ther dide, certeyn so wrooth was she,
That she was out of alle charitee.
Hir coverchiefs ful fyne were of ground;
I dorste swere they weyeden ten pound
That on a Sonday weren upon hir heed.
Hir hosen weren of fyn scarlet reed,
Ful streite yteyd, and shoes ful moyste and newe,
Boold was hir face and fair and reed of hewe.
She was a worthy womman al hir lyve:
Housbondes at chirche dore she hadde fyve,
Withouten oother compaignye in youthe—
But therof nedeth nat to speke as nowthe.
And thries hadde she been at Jerusalem;
She hadde passed many a straunge strem;
At Rome she hadde been, and at Boloigne,
In Galice at Seint Jame, and at Coloigne;
She koude muche of wandrynge by the weye.
Gat-tothed was she, soothly for to seye.
Upon an amblere esily she sat,
Ywympled wel, and on hir heed an hat
As brood as is a bokeler or a targe;
A foot-mantel aboute hir hipes large,
And on hir feet a paire of spores sharpe.
In felaweshipe wel koude she laughe and carpe.
Of remedies of love she knew per chaunce,
For she koude of that art the olde daunce.
A good man was ther of religioun,
And was a povre Person of a toun,
But riche he was of holy thoght and werk.
He was also a lerned man, a clerk,

That Christ's gospel would truly preach;
And parishioners would he devoutly teach.
Benign he was, and wonderfully diligent,
And in adversity entirely patient;
And so he had proved many times.
Altogether loath was he to excommunicate for his tithes,
But rather would he give, without a doubt,
To his various poor parishioners
Of his collection, and also of his own income;
He could with little have sufficient.
Wide was his parish, and houses far apart,
But he did not neglect for rain or thunder,
In sickness or in trouble, to visit
The farthest in his parish, great and small,
On foot, with a staff in his hand.
This noble example to his sheep he gave
That first he practiced, and afterward he preached.
Out of the gospel he took those words,
And this figure of speech he added to it:
That if gold rust, what shall iron do?
For if a priest be foul, in whom we trust,
No wonder that an unlearned man will rust.
And shameful it is, let priests take note,
A befouled shepherd and a clean sheep.
Well ought a priest to set an example,
By his cleanliness, how his sheep should live.
He did not hire out his benefice,
And leave his sheep sunk in the mire,
And run to London, to Saint Paul's,
To apply for a place as a chanter for souls,
Or to be retained by a guild;
But lived at home, and guarded well his fold,
So that the wolf would do it no harm;
He was a shepherd, not a businessman.
And although he was holy and virtuous,
He was to sinners not merciless,
Nor in his speech disdainful or haughty,
But in his teaching quiet and kindly.
To lead people to heaven by uprightness
And good example was his ambition.
But if anyone were obstinate,
Whoever he were, of high or low degree,
He would reprove him sharply at the time.
A better priest I'm sure does not exist.

That Cristes gospel trewely wolde preche;
His parisshens devoutly wolde he teche.
Benygne he was and wonder diligent,
And in adversitee ful pacient;
And swich he was ypreved ofte sithes.
Ful looth were hym to cursen for his tithes,
But rather wolde he yeven, out of doute,
Unto his povre parisshens aboute
Of his offryng and eek of his substaunce;
He koude in litel thyng have suffisaunce.
Wyd was his parisshe, and houses fer asonder,
But he ne lefte nat for reyn ne thonder,
In siknesse nor in meschief, to visite
The ferreste in his parisshe, muche and lite,
Upon his feet, and in his hand a staf.
This noble ensample to his sheep he yaf
That first he wroghte, and afterward he taughte.
Out of the gospel he tho wordes caughte,
And this figure he added eek therto:
That if gold rust, what shal iren do?
For if a preest be foul, on whom we truste,
No wonder is a lewed man to ruste.
And shame it is, if a preest take keep:
A shiten shepherde and a clene sheep.
Wel oghte a preest ensample for to yive
By his clennesse how that his sheep sholde lyve.
He sette nat his benefice to hyre,
And leet his sheep encombred in the myre,
And ran to London, unto Seinte Poules,
To seken hym a chaunterie for soules,
Or with a bretherhede to been withholde;
But dwelte at hoom and kepte wel his folde,
So that the wolf ne made it nat myscarie;
He was a shepherde and noght a mercenarie.
And though, he holy were and vertuous,
He was to synful men nat despitous,
Ne of his speche daungerous ne digne,
But in his techyng discreet and benygne.
To drawen folk to hevene by fairnesse,
By good ensample—this was his bisynesse.
But it were any persone obstinat,
What so he were, of heigh or lowe estat,
Hym wolde he synbben sharply for the nonys.
A bettre preest I trowe ther nowher noon ys.

He expected no pomp or reverence,
Nor considered himself above reproach,
But Christ's teaching, and that of his twelve apostles,
He taught, but first he followed it himself.
With him there was a Plowman, his brother,
That had carted many a load of dung;
A true worker and good was he,
Living in peace and perfect charity.
God loved he best with all his whole heart
At all times, whether he prospered or suffered,
And then his neighbour exactly as himself.
He would thrash, and also ditch and dig,
For Christ's sake, for every poor person,
Without pay, if it lay in his power.
His tithes he paid fairly and squarely,
Both on his own work and his property.
In working clothes he rode upon a mare.
There was also a Reeve and a Miller,
A Summoner and a Pardoner also,
A Manciple and myself—there were no more.
The Miller was a stout fellow (to treat him now);
Large of muscle, and of bones too.
That had been fully proved, for wherever he went,
At wrestling he would always win the prize.
He was short-armed, broad, and thickly built,
There was no door he could not heave off its hinges,
Or break it, by running at it with his head.
His beard was as red as any sow or fox,
And as broad as if it were a spade.
Right on the tip of his nose he had
A wart, and on it was a tuft of hair,
Red as the bristles of a sow's ears;
His nostrils were black and large.
A sword and buckler bore he by his side.
His mouth was as large as a large furnace.
He was a loose talker and a ribald joker,
Mostly concerning sin and indecent stories.
Well could he steal corn and charge treble;
And yet he had a thumb of gold, by heaven.
A white coat and a blue hood wore he.
He could play the bagpipe well,
And with it he accompanied us out of town.
A gentle Manciple was there from an Inn of Court,
From whom buyers might take example

He wayted after no pompe and reverence,
Ne maked him a spiced conscience,
But Cristes loore and his Apostles twelve
He taughte, but first he folwed it hymselve.
With hym ther was a Plowman, was his brother,
That hadde ylad of dong ful many a fother;
A trewe swynkere and a good was he,
Lyvyng in pees and parfit charitee.
God loved he best with al his hoole herte
At alle tymes, thogh him gamed or smerte,
And thanne his neighebore right as hymselve.
He wolde thresshe, and therto dyke and delve,
For Cristes sake, for every povre wight,
Withouten hire, if it lay in his myght.
His tithes payed he ful faire and wel,
Bothe of his propre swynk and his catel.
In a tabard he rood upon a mere.
Ther was also a Reve and a Millere,
A Somnour and a Pardoner also,
A Maunciple and myself—ther were namo.
The Millere was a stout carl for the nones;
Ful big he was of brawn and eek of bones.
That proved wel, for over al ther he cam,
At wrastlynge he wolde have alwey the ram.
He was short-sholdred, brood, a thikke knarre;
Ther was no dore that he nolde heve of harre,
Or breke it at a rennyng with his heed.
His berd as any sowe or fox was reed,
And therto brood, as though it were a spade.
Upon the cop right of his nose he hadde
A werte, and theron stood a tuft of herys,
Rede as the bristles of a sowes erys;
His nosethirles blake were and wyde.
A swerd and bokeler bar he by his syde.
His mouth as greet was as a greet forneys.
He was a janglere and a goliardeys,
And that was moost of synne and harlotries.
Wel koude he stelen corn and tollen thries;
And yet he hadde a thombe of gold, pardee.
A whit cote and a blew hood wered he.
A baggepipe wel koude he blowe and sowne,
And therwithal he broghte us out of towne.
A gentil Maunciple was ther of a temple,
Of which achatours myghte take exemple

To learn wisdom in buying provisions;
For whether he paid by cash, or by credit,
Always he marketed so carefully,
That he was always ahead and in a good position.
Now is not that a fair mercy of God,
That such a common man's knowledge shall exceed
The wisdom of a heap of learned men?
Of masters had he more than three times ten,
That were in law expert and skilful,
Of whom there were a dozen in that house
Capable of being stewards of incomes and estates
Of any lord that is in England,
To enable him to live on his income
Honorably and without debt, unless he were mad,
Or live as frugally as he might want,
And able to help a whole shire
In any mischance that might occur;
And yet this Manciple could outwit them all!
  The Reeve was a slender choleric man.
His beard was shaven as close as possible;
His hair was cut high around his ears;
He was clipped short in front like a priest;
His legs were very long and lean,
Like a stick, no calf was visible.
Well could he maintain a granary and bin;
No inspector could get the better of him.
He could predict by the drought and by the rain
The yield of his seed and grain.
His lord's sheep, his cattle, his dairy,
His swine, his horses, his stock and his poultry
Were wholly in this Reeve's care,
And by agreement he had submitted his accounts,
Ever since his lord was twenty years old.
No man could find him in arrears.
There was no supervisor, herdsman or other servant,
Whose cunning and trickery he didn't know;
They were as frightened of him as of the plague.
His home was in a fair countryside,
With green trees shading the place.
He was a better buyer than his lord.
He had accumulated private wealth.
He knew subtle ways of pleasing his lord,
Giving and loaning him of his own goods,
And receiving thanks, and also a coat and hood.

For to been wise in byyinge of vitaille;
For wheither that he payde or took by taille,
Algate he wayted so in his achaat,
That he was ay biforn and in good staat.
Now is nat that of God a ful fair grace,
That swich a lewed mannes wit shal pace
The wisdom of an heep of lerned men?
Of maistres hadde he mo than thries ten,
That were of lawe expert and curious,
Of whiche ther were a dozeyne in that hous
Worthy to been stywardes of rente and lond
Of any lord that is in Engelond,
To make him lyve by his propre good
In honour detteless but if he were wood,
Or lyve as scarsly as hym list desire,
And able for to helpen al a shire
In any caas that myghte falle or happe;
And yet this Maunciple sette hir aller cappe!
The Reve was a sclendre colerik man.
His berd was shave as neigh as ever he kan;
His heer was by his erys ful round yshorn;
His top was dokked lyk a preest biforn;
Ful longe were his legges and ful lene,
Ylik a staf, ther was no calf ysene.
Wel koude he kepe a gerner and a bynne;
Ther was noon auditour koude on him wynne.
Wel wiste he by the droghte and by the reyn
The yelding of his seed and of his greyn.
His lordes sheep, his neet, his dayerye,
His swyn, his hors, his stoor, and his pultrye
Was hoolly in this Reves governyng,
And by his covenant yaf the rekenyng,
Syn that his lord was twenty yeer of age.
Ther koude no man brynge hym in arrerage.
Ther nas baillif, hierde, nor oother hyne,
That he ne knew his sleighte and his covyne;
They were adrad of hym as of the deeth.
His wonyng was ful faire upon an heeth;
With grene trees yshadwed was his place.
He koude bettre than his lord purchace.
Ful riche he was astored pryvely.
His lord wel koude he plesen subtilly,
To yeve and lene hym of his owene good,
And have a thank, and yet a cote and hood.

In youth he had learned a good trade:
He was a right good worker, a carpenter.
This Reeve sat upon a very good stallion,
That was all dappled grey and named Scot.
A long upper-coat of Persian blue he wore,
And at his side he bore a rusty blade.
From Norfolk was this Reeve of whom I speak,
Near a town men call Baldeswell.
He was girdled up like a friar,
And always he rode last in our group.
There was a Summoner with us in that place,
Who had a fire-red cherubim's face,
For pimpled he was, with narrow eyes.
And hot he was, and lecherous as a sparrow,
With scabby black brows and scraggly beard;
Of his visage children were afraid.
There was no quicksilver, lead oxide or brimstone,
Borax, white lead, nor cream of tartar,
Nor cleansing and caustic ointment,
That could cure him of his white pimples,
Nor of the lumps sitting on his cheeks.
Well loved he garlic, onions, and also leeks,
And to drink strong wine, red as blood.
Then would he talk and shout as if he were mad;
And when he had drunk wine heavily,
Then would he speak no word but Latin.
He knew a few terms, two or three,
Which he had learned from some decree—
No wonder at that, he heard it all day long,
And you yourself know how a jay
Can say "Wat" as well as the pope can—
But if anyone questioned him on anything else,
Then he had exhausted all his learning;
Constantly *"Questio quid juris"* would he cry.
He was a gentle rascal and a kind one;
A better companion could not be found;
He would allow, for a quart of wine,
A good fellow to have his mistress
For twelve months, and excuse him fully.
But he could also take advantage of a girl.
And if he found anywhere a good fellow,
He would teach him to have no fear
In an affair of excommunication,
Unless a man's soul were in his purse,

In youthe he hadde lerned a good myster:
He was a wel good wrighte, a carpenter.
This Reve sat upon a ful good stot,
That was a pomely grey and highte Scot.
A long surcote of pers upon he hade,
And by his syde he baar a rusty blade.
Of Northfolk was this Reve of which I telle,
Biside a toun men clepen Baldeswelle.
Tukked he was as is a frere aboute,
And evere he rood the hyndreste of oure route.
A Somnour was ther with us in that place,
That hadde a fyr-reed cherubynnes face,
For sawcefleem he was, with eyen narwe.
And hoot he was, and lecherous as a sparwe,
With scaled browes blake and piled berd;
Of his visage children were aferd.
Ther nas quyksilver, lytarge, ne brymstoon,
Boras, ceruce, ne oille of tartre noon,
Ne oinement that wolde clense and byte,
That hym myghte helpen of his whelkes white,
Nor of the knobbes sittynge on his chekes.
Wel loved he garlek, oynons, and eek lekes,
And for to drynken strong wyn reed as blood.
Thanne wolde he speke and crye as he were wood;
And whan that he wel dronken hadde the wyn,
Thanne wolde he speke no word but Latyn.
A fewe termes hadde he, two or thre,
That he had lerned out of som decree—
No wonder is, he herde it al the day,
And eek ye knowen wel how that a jay
Kan clepen "Watte" as wel as kan the Pope—
But whoso koude in oother thyng hym grope,
Thanne hadde he spent al his philosophie;
Ay *"Questio quid juris"* wolde he crie.
He was a gentil harlot and a kynde;
A bettre felawe sholde men noght fynde;
He wolde suffre, for a quart of wyn,
A good felawe to have his concubyn
A twelf monthe, and excuse hym atte fulle.
Ful prively a fynch eek koude he pulle.
And if he foond owher a good felawe,
He wolde techen him to have noon awe
In swich caas of the Ercedekenes curs,
But if a mannes soule were in his purs,

In that case his purse should be punished.
"The purse is the archdeacon's hell", said he.
But well I know he most certainly lied;
Excommunication should be the dread of guilty men,
For excommunication will kill as absolution saves,
And also let him beware of a *Significavit.*
In his own way he had control
Over the young people of the diocese,
And knew their secrets, and was their adviser.
A garland he wore on his head
As large as an alehouse sign;
A round loaf of bread was his buckler.
With him there rode a gentle Pardoner
Of Rouncival, his friend and comrade,
Who had come straight from the court of Rome.
Full loudly he sang "Come hither, love, to me!"
The Summoner joined him with a strong bass;
Never was there trumpet half so loud.
This Pardoner had hair as yellow as wax,
But it hung smooth as does a hank of flax;
Such locks as he had hung down thinly,
And with them he covered his shoulders;
But sparsely it lay, by shreds here and there.
But, for amusement, he wore no hood,
For it was packed in his bag;
He thought he rode in the latest style;
With hair loose and bareheaded except for his cap.
He had shining eyes like a hare's.
He had a veronica sewed upon his cap.
His bag lay before him on his lap,
Brimful of pardons, come from Rome all hot.
A voice he had as tiny as a goat's;
No beard had he, nor ever would have;
As smooth he was as if he had been shaved;
I believe he was a gelding or a mare.
But in his occupation, from Berwick to Ware,
There was not another such pardoner.
For in his bag he had a pillowcase,
Which he said was Our Lady's veil;
He said he had a small piece of the sail
That Saint Peter had when he walked
Upon the sea, until Jesus Christ rescued him.
He had a cross of brass, full of gems,
And in a glass he had pig's bones.

For in his purs he sholde ypunysshed be.
"Purs is the Ercedekenes helle," saide he.
But wel I woot he lyed right in dede;
Of cursyng oghte ech gilty man him drede,
For curs wol slee right as assoillyng savith,
And also war him of a *Significavit*.
In daunger hadde he at his owene gise
The yonge girles of the diocise,
And knew hir conseil, and was al hir reed.
A gerland hadde he set upon his heed
As greet as it were for an ale-stake;
A bokeler hadde he maad him of a cake.
With hym ther rood a gentil Pardoner
Of Rouncival, his freend and his compeer,
That streight was comen fro the court of Rome.
Ful loude he soong, "Com hider, love, to me!"
This Somnour bar to hym a stif burdoun;
Was nevere trompe of half so greet a soun.
This Pardoner hadde heer as yelow as wex,
But smothe it heeng as dooth a strike of flex;
By ounces henge his lokkes that he hadde,
And therwith he his shuldres overspradde;
But thynne it lay, by colpons, oon and oon.
But hood for jolitee wered he noon,
For it was trussed up in his walet;
Hym thoughte he rood al of the newe jet;
Dischevelee save his cappe he rood al bare.
Swiche glarynge eyen hadde he as an hare.
A vernycle hadde he sowed upon his cappe.
His walet lay biforn hym in his lappe,
Bretful of pardon, comen from Rome al hoot.
A voys he hadde as smal as hath a goot;
No berd hadde he, ne nevere sholde have;
As mothe it was as it were late yshave;
I trowe he were a geldyng or a mare.
But of his craft, fro Berwyk into Ware,
Ne was ther swich another pardoner.
For in his male he hadde a pilwe-beer,
Which that he seyde was Oure Lady veyl;
He seyde he hadde a gobet of the seyl
That Seint Peter hadde whan that he wente
Upon the see, til Jhesu Crist hym hente.
He hadde a croys of laton, ful of stones,
And in a glas he hadde pigges bones.

But with these relics, whenever he found
A poor parson living in the country,
Within a day he took in more money
Than the parson got in two months;
And thus with feigned sincerity and tricks,
He made monkeys out of the parson and his people.
But to tell the truth, all in all,
He was in church a noble ecclesiastic;
He knew how to read a lesson or a story,
But best of all he sang an offertory;
For well he knew when that song was sung,
He must preach and sharpen his tongue
To win silver, as he well knew how;
Therefore he sung so merrily and loud.
   Now I have told you truly, in brief,
The status, the dress, the number, and also the cause
Of the gathering of this company
In Southwark at this fine inn
Called the Tabard, close to the Bell.
But now it is time to tell you
What we did that same night.
On which we came to that inn;
And afterwards I will tell of our journey,
And the remainder of our pilgrimage.
But first I beg you out of your courtesy,
That you do not ascribe it to my ill breeding,
Even though I speak plainly in this narration,
To tell you their words and their behaviour,
Even though I repeat their exact words.
For this you know as well as I:
Whoever tells another man's story,
Must reproduce, as exactly as he can,
Every word, if his memory serves,
However crude and free his language,
Or else he tells his tale untruly,
Or invent things, or find new words.
He may spare no one, not even his brother;
He is as bound to say one word as another.
Christ Himself spoke broadly enough in holy writ,
And you know well that it is not immoral.
Plato also says, for those who can read him,
That words should be cousin to the deed.
Also I beg you to forgive me,
If I have not placed people in their rank,

But with thise relikes whan that he fond
A povre person dwellynge upon lond,
Upon a day he gat hym moore moneye
Than that the person gat in monthes tweye;
And thus with feyned flaterye and japes,
He made the person and the peple his apes.
But trewely to tellen atte laste,
He was in chirche a noble ecclesiaste;
Wel koude he rede a lesson or a storie,
But alderbest he song an offertorie;
For wel he wiste whan that song was songe,
He moste preche and wel affile his tonge
To wynne silver, as he ful wel koude;
Therefore he song the murierly and loude.
  Now have I told you soothly, in a clause,
Th'estaat, th'array, the nombre, and eek the cause
Why that assembled was this compaignye
In Southwerk at this gentil hostelrye
That highte the Tabard, faste by the Belle.
But now is tyme to yow for to telle
How that we baren us that ilke nyght,
Whan we were in that hostelrie alyght;
And after wol I telle of our viage
And al the remenaunt of oure pilgrimage.
But first I pray yow of youre curteisye,
That ye n'arette it nat my vileynye,
Thogh that I pleynly speke in this matere,
To telle yow hir wordes and hir cheere,
Ne thogh I speke hir wordes proprely.
For this ye knowen al so wel as I:
Who so shal telle a tale after a man,
He moot reherce, as neigh as evere he kan,
Everich a word, if it be in his charge,
Al speke he never so rudeliche and large,
Or ellis he moot telle his tale untrewe,
Or feyne thyng, or fynde wordes newe.
He may nat spare althogh he were his brother;
He moot as wel seye o word as another.
Crist spak hymself ful brode in holy writ,
And wel ye woot no vileynye is it.
Eek Plato seith, whoso kan him rede,
The wordes mote be cosyn to the dede.
Also I pray yow to foryeve it me,
Al have I nat set folk in hir degree

Here in this tale in the order that they should be.
My brains are weak, you can well understand.
Our Host gave each of us a great welcome,
And set us down to supper forthwith.
He served us with the best of food;
Strong was the wine, and we were in a mood to drink.
Our Host was a man altogether fit
To have been a marshall in a dining hall.
A large man he was, with bright eyes;
There was no finer citizen in Cheapside,
Bold of speech, and sensible, and well educated,
And he lacked nothing of real manhood.
As well as this he was a merry man,
And after supper he began to jest,
And spoke of pleasure among other things,
After we had settled our bills,
And spoke thus, "Now, gentlemen, truly,
You are heartily welcome here;
For by my troth, if I don't tell a lie,
I have not seen this year so merry a company
At once in this inn as at present.
I should like to provide pleasure for you, if I knew how.
And a pastime has just occurred to me
To give you pleasure, and it will cost nothing.
You go to Canterbury—God speed you;
May the blessed martyr reward you.
And well I know as you go along,
You plan to tell tales and amuse yourselves,
For truly, there is no comfort nor mirth
In riding along silent as a stone;
And therefore I shall create a diversion,
As I said before, and give you some comfort.
And if you all agree, by common consent,
To be ruled by my judgement,
And to proceed as I shall explain,
Tomorrow when you go on your way,
Now by my father's soul who is dead,
If you are not merry I will give you my head!
Hold up your hands without more talk."
Our decision was not hard to find;
We did not think it worth deliberating over,
And agreed with him without further consideration,
And asked him to give his verdict as it pleased him.
"Gentlemen," he said, "now listen with good will;

Here in this tale as that they sholde stonde.
My wit is short, ye may wel understonde.
  Greet cheere made oure Hoost us everichon,
And to the soper sette he us anon.
He served us with vitaille at the beste;
Strong was the wyn, and wel to drynke us leste.
A semely man oure Hooste was withalle
For to been a marchal in an halle.
A large man he was, with eyen stepe;
A fairer burgeys was ther noon in Chepe,
Boold of his speche, and wys, and wel ytaught,
And of manhood hym lakkede right naught.
Eek therto he was right a murye man,
And after soper pleyen he bigan,
And spak of myrthe amonges othere thynges,
Whan that we hadde maad oure rekenynges,
And seyde thus, "Now, lordynges, trewely,
Ye been to me right welcome, hertely;
For by my trouthe, if that I shal nat lye,
I saugh nat this yeer so murye a compaignye
At ones in this herberwe as is now.
Fayn wolde I doon yow myrthe, wiste I how.
And of a myrthe I am right now bythoght
To doon yow ese, and it shal coste noght.
Ye goon to Caunterbury—God yow speede;
The blisful martir quite yow youre meede.
And wel I woot as ye goon by the weye,
Ye shapen yow to talen and to pleye,
For trewely, confort ne myrthe is noon
To ride by the weye domb as a stoon;
And therfore wol I maken yow disport,
As I seyde erst, and doon yow som confort.
And if yow liketh alle, by oon assent,
For to stonden at my juggement,
And for to werken as I shal yow seye,
Tomorwe whan ye riden by the weye,
Now by my fader soule that is deed,
But ye be murye I wol yeve yow myn heed!
Hoolde up youre hondes withouten moore speche."
  Oure conseil was nat longe for to seche;
Us thoughte it was nat worth to make it wys,
And graunted hym withouten moore avys,
And bad him seye his voirdit as hym leste.
  "Lordynges," quod he, "now herkneth for the beste;

And take it not, I beg you, disdainfully.
This is the point, to speak briefly and plainly,
That each of you, to shorten our way
On this journey, shall tell two tales—
En route to Canterbury, I mean to say—
And two more on the way homeward,
Of adventures that have once happened;
And whichever of you does the best of all—
That is to say, that tells in this contest
The most significant and amusing tales—
Shall be given dinner at the expense of all,
Here in this place, sitting by this post,
When we return from Canterbury.
And to make you more merry,
I will myself gladly ride with you,
Even at my own expense, and be your guide;
And whoever opposes my judgment
Shall pay all that we spend along the way.
And if you promise that it will be so,
Tell me at once, without more words,
And I will prepare myself accordingly."
This thing was granted and our oaths sworn
With entirely glad hearts, and we begged him too
That he would agree to do his part,
And that he would be our director,
And remember and judge our tales,
And plan a dinner at a certain price,
And we would be ruled by his direction
In great and small things; and thus by general consent
We fell in with his plan.
And at that the wine was quickly fetched;
And we drank and each went to bed,
Without any further delay.
Next morning when day began to break,
Up rose our Host and was rooster for us all,
And gathered us together in a flock,
And forth we rode, slightly faster than a walk,
As far as the watering-place of Saint Thomas;
And there our Host slowed down his horse,
And said, "Gentlemen, listen if you please.
You know your agreement and I remind you of it;
If evening and morning are in agreement,
Let us see now who shall tell the first tale.
If ever again I drink wine or ale,

But taak it noght, I prey yow, in desdeyn.
This is the poynt, to speken short and pleyn,
That ech of yow, to shorte with oure weye
In this viage, shal telle tales tweye—
To Caunterbury-ward, I mene it so—
And homward he shal tellen othere two,
Of aventures that whilom have bifalle;
And which of yow that bereth hym best of alle—
That is to seyn, that telleth in this caas
Tales of best sentence and moost solaas—
Shal have a soper at oure aller cost,
Here in this place, sittynge by this post,
Whan that we come agayn fro Caunterbury.
And for to make yow the moore mury,
I wol myselven goodly with yow ryde,
Right at myn owene cost, and be youre gyde;
And who so wole my juggement withseye
Shal paye al that we spenden by the weye.
And if ye vouche sauf that it be so,
Tel me anon, withouten wordes mo,
And I wol erly shape me therfore."
 This thyng was graunted and oure othes swore
With ful glad herte, and preyden hym also
That he wolde vouche sauf for to do so,
And that he wolde been oure governour,
And of oure tales juge and reportour,
And sette a soper at a certeyn pris,
And we wol reuled been at his devys
In heigh and lowe; and thus by oon assent
We been acorded to his juggement.
And therupon the wyn was fet anon;
We dronken and to reste wente echon,
Withouten any lenger taryynge.
 Amorwe whan that day bigan to sprynge,
Up roos oure Hoost and was oure aller cok,
And gadred us togidre in a flok,
And forth we riden, a litel moore than paas,
Unto the wateryng of Seint Thomas;
And there oure Hoost bigan his hors areste,
And seyde, "Lordynges, herkneth if yow leste.
Ye woot youre forward and I it yow recorde;
If even-song and morwe-song accorde,
Lat see now who shal telle the firste tale.
As evere mote I drynke wyn or ale,

Whoever rebels against my decision
Shall pay for all that by the way is spent.
Now draw lots, before we go farther;
Whoever draws the shortest shall begin.
Sir Knight," said he, "my master and my lord,
Now draw your lot, for that is my ruling.
Come closer," said he, "my lady Prioress,
And you, sir Clerk, forget your bashfulness,
Do not deliberate. Hands out, every man!"
And so everyone began to draw,
And to speak briefly, as it happened,
Whether by adventure or luck or chance,
The fact is this, the lot fell to the Knight,
Which was pleasing to everyone,
And tell his tale he must, as was right,
By agreement and according to plan,
As you have heard. Why use more words?
And when this good man saw that it was so,
Since he was wise and willing
To keep his agreement by free consent,
He said, "Since I am to begin the game,
Why, welcome be the lot, in God's name."
Now let us ride, and listen to what I say."
And with that word we rode forth on our way,
And he began in great good spirits
His tale at once, and said what you may hear.

Who so be rebel to my juggement
Shal paye for al that by the wey is spent.
Now draweth cut er that we ferrer twynne;
He which that hath the shorteste shal bigynne.
"Sire Knyght," quod he, "my mayster and my lord,
Now draweth cut, for that is myn accord.
Cometh neer," quod he, "my lady Prioresse,
And ye, sire Clerk, lat be youre shamefastnesse,
Ne studieth noght. Ley hond to, every man!"
Anon to drawen every wight bigan,
And shortly for to tellen as it was,
Were it by aventure or sort or cas,
The sothe is this, the cut fil to the Knyght,
Of which ful blithe and glad was every wight,
And telle he moste his tale, as was resoun,
By forward and by composicioun,
As ye han herd. What nedeth wordes mo?
And whan this goode man saugh that it was so,
As he that wys was and obedient
To kepe his forward by his free assent,
He seyde, "Syn I shal begynne the game,
What, welcome be the cut, a Goddes name!
Now lat us ryde, and herkneth what I seye."
And with that word we ryden forth oure weye,
And he bigan with right a murye cheere
His tale anon, and seyde as ye may heere.

NOTES

LINE

3 **veyne:** sap-duct. **licour:** life-giving moisture.

4. **vertu:** here, the power to make grow.

5. **Zephyrus:** the west wind, often associated with spring.

8. **Ram:** the first division, or sign, of the zodiac (Aries), hence the sun is called "yonge," since it has only entered the first stage of its annual course (March-April).

10-11. i.e., springtime amorousness causes the birds to sing all night.

13. **palmeres:** pilgrims, so called from the palms that they carried.

15. **shires:** one of the political-geopraphical divisions of England.

16. **Caunterbury:** site of the shirne of St. Thomas.

17. **martir:** Archbishop Thomas Becket, whose feud with King Henry II led to his murder in 1170. The scene of this martyrdom was the object of pilgrimages for centuries afterward.

20. **Southwerk:** a borough of London on the south side of the Thames.
Tabard: an inn, identified by a sign showing a "tabard," a short coat worn over armor. The plowman on the pilgrimage is wearing a "tabard" (see 541).

45. **To riden out:** i.e., take the field, go on military expeditions.
chivalrye: knighthood.

46. **curteisye:** in addition to modern meaning of courtesy, the word in the Middle Ages implies the manners supposed to belong to the court.

51. **Alisaundre:** Alexandria, captured by King Peter of Cyprus in 1365. The battles which follow indicate the Knight's long and distinguished military career. All the campaigns were against the infidels—Saracens, Turks, and pagans of north-eastern Europe (Russia and Lithuania).

58. **Lyeys . . . Satalye:** in Armenia and Asia Minor, respectively; both were taken by Peter of Cyprus.

62. **Tramyssene:** or Tlemcen, was in Algeria.

63. **lystes:** listes or tournaments, meaning single combat against the enemy

79. **Squier:** esquire, whose candidacy for knighthood includes attending upon a knight, as here.

86. **Flaundres . . .:** a reference to the expeditions into Flanders, Artois, and Picardy as a part of the war between the rival popes of Rome and Avignon.

100. **carf biforn . . .:** a squire performed this function for the knight he served.

101. **Yeman:** a yeoman ranked above the groom in the service of the knight, and from the description seems to have fulfilled the function of game warden.
he: i.e., the Knight.

104. **pecock arwes:** arrows feathered with peacock feathers.

115. **Cristophre:** the medal of St. Christopher, patron saint of foresters.

118. **Prioresse:** a nun who is the superior of a priory.

LINE

125. **Stratford atte Bowe:** about two miles outside of London, where there was the priory of St. Leonard's, with nine nuns and a prioress. While there was no real need for anyone in England to speak French in 1387, the language was probably cultivated at St. Leonard's because of its former aristocratic associations.

132. **curteisie:** the Prioress' table manners were those of a lady of fashion.

151. **wympel:** the wimple was a garment covering the head, sides of the face, and neck.

159. **gauded:** having larger, dividing beads of green.

162. **Amor vincit omnia:** love conquers all.

163. **Another Nonne:** The Prioress naturally traveled with a companion. The chaplain was a kind of administrative assistant to the Prioress.

166. **outridere:** an outrider was a monk whose duty was to oversee the monastery's estates.

173. **reule of . . .** the rules of monastic discipline established by St. Maurus and taken from St. Benedict and the Benedictine order.

194. **grys:** gray fur, from the squirrel, was the most expensive sort.

207. **palfrey:** saddle horse.

208. **Frere:** The Friar was a member of one of the four begging orders, but Chaucer does not tell us which; these orders were often criticized in Chaucer's day.

209. **lymytour:** one assigned a certain area in which to beg.

213. **owene cost:** possible because they had been his mistresses.

216. **frankeleyns:** rich farmers, who are more fully described below, 331 ff.

218-20. i.e., he was empowered by his order to hear confessions and give absolution in cases beyond the jurisdiction of a parish priest.

233-34. **knyves and pynnes:** Wycliffe attacked the friars for becoming peddlers of knives, pins, purses, etc., and for giving them to women.

236. **rote:** a fiddle, or stringed instrument resembling a lyre.

238. **nekke whit:** regarded in the Middle Ages as a mark of sensuality.

242. **lazar:** leper (from Lazarus), but here probably any poor or diseased person.

254. **In principio:** "in the beginning (was the word)," the opening words of the Gospel of St. John and a favourite greeting among friars.

258. **love-dayes:** these were days appointed for settling suits out of court.

259. **cloysterer:** a poor brother who remained in the cloister.

270. **forked berd:** in Chaucer's day, one of the fashionable ways of wearing a beard.

271. **mottelee:** cloth woven with mixed colors.

277. Middleburgh was a port in the low countries, and Orwell a river in Suffolk.

278. This foreign exchange of currency was illegal.

285. **Clerk:** at Oxford, an ecclesiastical student.

286. i.e., he had studied logic, which was part of his qualifications for the B.A.

291. **benefice:** appointment to the rectorship of a parish church.

LINE

294. **Twenty bookes:** a large library at this time.

297. **philosophre:** the word also meant alchemist, and this is a pun on that second meaning.

309. **Sergeant:** a lawyer of the highest degree, chosen from the most eminent senior members of the bar.

310. **Parvys:** this was the porch of St. Paul's cathedral, a favorite place for lawyers to congregate, and perhaps meet clients.

314. **assise:** the regular county court.

315. **patente:** letter of appointment from the king.
commissioun: commissioned to hear cases of all sorts.

319. **fee symple:** a title of ownership without restriction.

331. **Frankeleyn:** a well-to-do landholder.

336. The philosophy of Epicurus was held to recommend luxurious living.

340. **Saint Julian:** patron saint of hospitality.

356. **knyght of the shire:** the representative of the county in parliament.

361. **Haberdasshere:** a seller of hats, needles, buttons, etc.

362. **Tapycer:** upholsterer or tapestry maker.

364. One of the parish guilds, a religious and fraternal organization.

370. The dais was reserved for the mayor and aldermen.

376. The wives of aldermen assumed the title "lady."

377. **vigilies:** ceremonial processions on the eve of festivals; the aldermen's wives headed the procession.

389. **Dertemouthe:** Dartmouth in the southwest was a large port in the Middle Ages.

395. **good felawe:** the expression was sometimes used ironically, for "rascal," which seems to be the intention here.

404. **Hulle to Cartage:** Hull, in Yorkshire, and probably Cartagena, in Spain, rather than Carthage.

408. **Gootlond:** an island in the Baltic near Sweden. Fynystere; on the west coast of Spain.

414. **astronomye:** the influence of the stars, our astrology, was considered most important in the practice of medicine.

420. These were the qualities, or "humours"—also called the sanguine, phlegmatic, choleric, and melancholy—the proper balance of which in the body was necessary to health.

429-34. The men here mentioned were the authors of the chief medical textbooks of the Middle Ages.

438. Physicians were held to be skeptics.

448. Ypres and Gaunt were Flemish towns noted for their fine fabrics.

450. The parishoners came forward in order of rank.

460. In the Middle Ages marriages were performed at the church door.

463. **Jerusalem:** pronounced as three distinct syllables.

465-66. As well as the Holy Sepulchre at Jerusalem, the Wife of Bath had visited the other famous shrines at Rome, Boulogne, St. James of Compostella in Galicia, and Cologne.

LINE

475. **remedies of love:** the phrase was associated with the Latin poet Ovid's Remedia Amoris.

486. Excommunicate in order to force payment of tithes.

489. **substance:** his own income, derived from his benefice and from tithes.

497. i.e., he practiced what he preached.

500. i.e., if the highest should weaken, what would the lowest do?

507. This was a not uncommon practice; a priest might engage a substitute in his own parish, and become a chantry priest in London (see 510).

511. To be retained as priest by a guild was also an easy and lucrative position.

560. **goliardeys:** the wandering scholars of the twelfth century were known as Goliards, from their leader, Golias. Their poems and songs in Latin were satirical and often indecent.

563. From the proverb "An honest miller has a thumb of gold," meaning that there were no honest millers.

567. **Maunciple:** a manciple was a minor employee of an institution, whose principal functions was to purchase provisions.
temple: an Inn of Court. There were four in London—Lincoln's Inn, Gray's Inn, the Inner Temple, and the Middle Temple, the last two taking their names from their buildings, which had belonged to the Knights Templars. They each had about two hundred students who studied common law and liberal arts. Many had no intention of becoming lawyers, but wanted to be able to look after their properties.

579. **stywardes:** a steward was the chief officer of the manor of a lord, and supervised in his absence.

587. **Reve:** the Reeve was attached to the manor to supervise produce and work, and keep the accounts.

611. **his:** i.e., the lord's.

623. **Somnour:** a summoner was an officer who cited persons to appear in court. In the fourteenth century he was also an officer of the archdeacon, and presided over the archdeacon's court, which had jurisdiction in matrimonial cases and in moral offenses such as adultery and fornication. Bribery was not unknown and other sources beside Chaucer attribute corruption to the summoner.

624. **fyr-reed:** cherubs were traditionally painted with red faces in the Middle Ages.

626. Sparrows were proverbially lecherous; the bird was often associated with Venus.

643. **Watte:** jays were taught to say "Wat," a diminutive of Walter.

646. **Questio . . .** "the question is, what law applies"? a common legal expression.

655. **Ercedekenes curs:** archdeacon's curse, i.e., excommunication.

662. **Significavit:** the opening word in the writ issued by the authorities to seize a convicted party.

LINE

664. **girles:** the word may mean young people of either sex.

667. **ale-stake:** a horizontal pole extending out from an alehouse, with a garland on the end.

669. **Pardoner:** a man authorized to sell papal indulgences, in lieu of other forms of penance. Pardoners were often satirized and criticized for dishonesty.

670. **Rouncival:** a convent near Charing Cross, then on the edge of London.

672. Probably a line in a popular song.

685. **vernycle:** a veronica was a copy of St. Veronica's handkerchief, given by her to Christ carrying the cross. It was said to have received the imprint of his face.

692. The phrase means from one end of England to the other.

698. **hym hente:** the reference is either to Christ's extending a helping hand to Peter when the latter walked on the water and became afraid or to the fact that Peter was a fisherman before joining Christ.

709. **lesson:** passage from the Bible or the Fathers read in the service; a "storie" is several such connected lessons.

710. **offertorie:** a chant preparatory to the ceremonial offering of the Bread and Wine, at which time the people made their offerings.

719. **the Belle:** another tavern.

752. **marchal:** the marshall was the person of authority in serving meals. He directed the servants and quelled disturbances if necessary.

754. **Chepe:** Cheapside, a main thoroughfare in Chaucer's London, and a centre of commerce.

794. The plan which calls for four tales from each pilgrim was never completed.

826. **wateryng:** a watering place for horses at the second milestone on the road to Canterbury.

GLOSSARY

Abbreviations used in Glossary

A.N.	Anglo-Norman.	**Lat.**	Latin.
Dan.	Danish.	**L.L.**	Late Latin.
Du.	Dutch.	**M.E.**	Middle English.
Ety. dub.	Etymology doubtful.	**M.H.G.**	Middle High German.
Gk.	Greek.	**O.E.**	Old English; Anglo-Saxon.
Icel.	Old Icelandic.	**O.F.**	Old French.
	O.H.G. Old High German.		

The meaning of other abbreviations used is obvious; e.g. pres. for Present Tense; p.p. for Past Participle.

N.B.—(1) Chaucer spells a word with either i or y.
(2) Consult the notes in association with the Glossary.

a: adj., any, 194; one, 703 (O.E. an).
a: prep., in, on, 854 (O.E. on).
able: adj., fit, 167; capable 584 (Lat. habilis; O.F. hable).
aboven: prep., above, 53 (O.E. abufan).
absolucioun: n., absolution, 222 (Lat. absolutionem).
accord: n., contract, decision, 838 (O.F. acord).
accordant: adj., in accordance with, 37 (O.F. acordant).
accorde: v., agree, 830; **acorded:** agreed, 818; suited, 244 (O.F. acorder).
achaat: purchasing, 571 (O.F. achat).
achatour: n., buyer of provisions, 568 (O.F. achatour).
adoun: adv., down, 393 (O.E. adune).
adrad: p.p. as adj., frightened, 605 (O.E. ondrædan).
adveritsee: n., adversity, 484 (Lat. adversitatem).
aferd: p.p. as adj., afraid, 628 (O.E. afæran).
affyle: v., soften, polish, 712 (O.F. affiler).
after: adv., afterwards, 162 (O.E. æfter).
after: prep., according to, 125 (O.E. æfter).
agayn: adv., back again, 801 (O.E. ongean).
agayn: prep., against, 66 (O.E. ongean).
al: adj. and pron. all; **alle,** pl., 96; **aller,** gen, pl. 799, 823 (O.E. eall, ealle, ealra).
al: adv., entirely, quite, 248 (O.E. eall).
al: conj., although, 734 (O.E. eall).
al be that: conj., although, 297 (O.E. eall + be + pæt).
alderbest: adv., best of all, 710 (O.E. ealra betst).
alderman: n., head of a guild, 372 (O.E. ealder-mann).
ale-stake: n., ale-stake, see note to 1. 667 (O.E. ealu-staca).
algate: adv., always, 571 (O.N. alla + gata).
alight: p.p., descended from horseback, 722 (O.E. alihtan).
aller: see **al,** adj.
als: adv., as, 170 (O.E. eal + swa).
almoost: adv., almost, 155 (O.E. eal + mœst).
al-so: adv., in additon, 64; conj., as, 730 (O.E. eal + swa).

alwey: adv., always, continually, 185 (O.E. eal + weg).
amblere: n., an, ambling horse, 469 (O.F. ambler).
amonges: prep., amongst, 759 (O.E. onmang + es).
amorwe: adv., on the next day, 822 (O.E. on + morgen).
amyable: adj., pleasant, amiable, 138 (O.F. amable).
anlaas, n., two-edged knife, dagger, 357 (Ety. dub.).
anon: at once, 32 (O.E. on + an).
anoon: see **anon.**
anoynt: p.p. anointed, 199 (O.F. enoint).
ape: n., ape, dupe, 706 (O.E. apa).
apothecarie: n., preparer of drugs, or medicines, 425 (L.L. apothecarium).
apyked: trimmed, 365; p.p. (O.F. piquer).
aqueyntaunce: n., acquaintance, 245 (O.F. acointance).
areste: v., stop, 827 (O.F. arester).
arette: v., attribute to, 726 (O.F. aretter).
aright: adv., wholly, 1896 aright as, just as, 267 (O.E. on riht).
armee: n., armed expedition, 60 (O.F. armee).
array: n., array, dress, equipment, 41 (O.F. arei).
arrerage: n., arrears, 602 (O.F. arrerage).
arwe: n., arrow, 107 (O.E. arwe).
aryse: v., accrue, arise, 219 (O.E. arisan).
ascendent: n., the degree of the imaginary celestial circle of the sun's orbit which is above the horizon at a given moment, 417. (Lat. ascendentem).
asonder: adj., scattered, 491 (O.E. on-sundran).
assent: n., consent, 777 (Lat. assentire).
assente: v., consent, agree to, 374 (Lat. assentire).
assoilyng, n., absolution, 661 (O.F. assoille).
astored, p.p., stocked, 609 (O.F. estorer).
astronomye: n., astrology, 414 (O.F. astronomic).
atte: prep. + adj., at the, 29 (O.E. œt + pœm).
avaunce: v., profit, 246 (O.F. avancier).
avaunt: n., boast, 227 (O.F. avanter).
aventure: n., luck, chance, accident, 25 (O.F. aventure).
avys: n., deliberation, 786 (O.F. avis).
awe: n., dread, fear, 654 (O.N. agi).
ay: adv., always, 63 (O.N. ei).

baar: see **bere.**
bacheler: n., a candidate for knighthood, 80 (O.F. bachelor < L.L. baccalarius).
bad: v., see **bidden.**
baggepipe: n., bagpipe, 565 (O.N. baggi + O.E. pipa).
baillif: n., bailiff, 603 (O.F. baillif).
bake: v., bake, 384, p.p., as adj., 343 (O.E. bacan).
bakemete: n., pies, pastries, 343 (O.E. bacen + mete).
balled: adj., bald, 193 (Ety. dub.).
bar: see **bere.**
bare: adj., uncovered, bare-headed, 683 (O.E. bær).
bargayne: n., bargain, 282 (O.F. bargaine).
barge: n., ship, 410 (O.F. barge).
barre: n., ornamental bands, 329 (Ety. dub.).
bataille: n., battle, 61 (O.F. bataille).
bathed: p.p. of bathe: v., bathe, 3.

bawdrik: n., baldric, a belt worn across the chest, 116 (O.H.G. balderich).
be: see **been.**
bedde: n., bed., 293 (O.E. bedd).
bede: n., bead of a rosary, 159 (O.E. bed).
been: v., to be. **ben:** also infin., 141; **beth, been:** pres. pl., 178, 762; **been:** p.p., 119; **be:** p.p., 60 (O.E. beon). **nas = ne was,** 251; past tense, **were, weren,** 28.
beggere: n., beggar man, 252 (O.F. begart).
beggestere: n., beggar woman, 242 (O.F. begart + estre (fem, suffix)).
ben: see **been.**
benefice: n., a cure of souls, a living, 291 (Lat. beneficium).
benygne: adj., kindly, 483 (O.F. benigne).
berd: n., beard, 270 (O.E. berd).
bere: v., bear, conduct. Pres. sing., 796 **bar:** past sing., 108; **baren:** past pl., 721; **born,** p.p., 87 (O.E. beran).
berye: n., berry, 207 (O.E. berige).
bet: adv., better, 242 (O.E. bet).
beth: see **been.**
bettre: adj., better, 256; adv., better, 342 (O.E. betera).
bevere: adj., made of the fur of the beaver, 272 (O.E. befer).
bidden: v., to command. **bit:** pres. sing., 187; **bad:** past tense, 787 (O.E. biddan).
bifalle: v., to happen. **bifel:** past sing., 19; **bifalle:** p.p. 795 (O.E. befeollan).
bifore: prep., before, 450; adv., in front of, 377 (O.E. be-foran).
biforn: adv., before, in front, 590; prep., in the presence of, 100 (O.E. be-foran).
bigynne: v., to begin, 42; **bigan:** past sing., 44; **bigonne:** p.p., 52 (O.E. beginnan).
biloved: adj., beloved, 215 (M.E. biluve(n) + ed).
bisette: v., employ. Past sing., 279 (O.E. bisettan).
bisily: adv., earnestly, 301 (O.E. bysig + lic).
bisiness: n., business, anxiety, attention, 520 (O.E. bisignis).
bismotered: p.p., solid, 76 (Ety. dub. Perhaps from "smut").
bisy: adj., busy, 321; **bisier:** adj., busier, 322 (O.E. bysig).
bisyde: prep., near, 620 (O.E. be-sidan).
bit: see **bidden.**
bitwixe: prep., between, 277 (O.E. betwix).
blade: n., sword, 618 (O.E. blæd).
blak: adj., black, 294 (O.E. blæc).
blame: v. ger., to be blamed, 375 (O.F. blâmer).
blankmanger: n., see note to 387 (O.F. blanc + manger).
blede: v., to bleed, past tense bledde, 145 (O.E. bledan).
blew: adj., blue, 564 (O.F. bleu).
blisful: adj., blessed, 17 (O.E. blios + ful).
blithe: adj., happy, glad, 846 (O.E. blioe).
boille: v., boil, 380 (O.F. boillir).
bokeler: n., buckler, small shield, 112 (O.F. boucler).
blood: adj., fearless, bold, 458 (O.E. bald).
boote: n., remedy, 424 (O.E. bot).
bootes: n., boots, 203 (O.F. bote).
boras: n., borax, 630 (O.F. boras).
bord: n., table, for meals, 52 (O.E. bord).
born: see **bere.**
bowe: n., longbow, 108 (O.E. boga).

bracer: n., guard for the wrist, used in archery, 111 (O.F. brasseure).
bras: n., brass, 366 (O.E. bræs).
brawn: n., muscle, 546 (O.F. braon).
breed: n., bread, 147 (O.E. bread).
breem: n., bream, a fresh-water fish, 350 (O.F. breame).
breeth: n., breath, 5 (O.E. bræo).
breken: v., smash, break to pieces, 551 (O.E. brecan).
brest: n., breast, 115 (O.E. breost).
bretful: adj., brimful, 687 (O.E. brerdful).
bretherhed: n., brotherhood, guild, fraternity, 511 (O.E. breor + et).
brimstoon: n., brimstone, sulphur, 629 (O.E. brennan(to burn) + stan).
brode: adv., plainly, without reserve, 739 (O.E. brade).
brooche: n., brooch, 160 (L.L. brocca).
brood: adj., broad, wide, 155 (O.E. brad).
broun: adj., brown, burnished, shining, 109 (O.E. brun).
brydel: n., bridle, 169 (O.E. bridel).
burdon: n., accompaniment, in the base, a drone, 673 (L.L. burdonem).
burgeys: n., citizen, burgess, 369 (O.F. burgeis).
but-if: conj., unless, 351 (O.E. butan + gif).
by: prep., on, 581 (O.E. bi).
by-cause: conj., because, 174 (O.E. bi + Lat. causam).
bynne: n., bin, for storing corn, 593 (O.E. binn).
byte: v., cauterise, 631 (O.E. bitan).
byyinge: n., purchasing, 569 (O.E. bycgyune).

caas: n., accident, case, 545; legal cases, 323 (O.F. cas).
cacchen: v., catch; past sing., caught, 145 (O.F. cachier).
cake: n., flat loaf of bread, cake, 668 (O.N. kaka).
calf: n., calf of the leg, 592 (O.N. kalfi).
cam: see **comen.**
can: see **connen.**
cappe: n., cap, 683 (O.E. cæppe).
carf: see **kerven.**
carl: n., fellow, 545 (O.N. karl).
carpe: v., chatter, 474 (O.N. karpa).
cas: see **caas.**
catel: n., property, possessions, 373; cattle, 540 (O.F. catel).
ceint: n., girdle, 329 (O.F. ceint).
celle: n., monastery dependent on a larger house, 172 (Lat. cellam).
certeinly: adv., certainly, 204 (O.F. certain + O.E. lic).
certeyn: adv., certainly, 375 (O.F. certain).
certeyn: adj., fixed, definite, 815 (O.F. certain).
ceruce: n., white lead, 630 (L.L. cerussam).
chambres: n., roms, 28 (O.F. chambre).
champioun: n., prize-fighter, 239 (O.F. champion).
chaped: p.p., mounted, capped, 366 (O.F. chape).
chapeleyne: n., female chaplain, secretary, 164 (O.F. chapelain).
chapman: n., merchant, trader, 397 (O.E. ceap + man).
charge: n., undertaking, responsibility, 733 (O.F. charge).
charitable: adj., sympathetic, 143 (O.F. charitable).
charitee: n., christian love, 452 (O.F. charite).
chaunged: past sing., changed, varied, 348 (O.F. changer).
chaunterie: n., chantry, fees for singing mass. (O.F. chanterie).

chekes: n., cheeks, 633 (O.E. cece).
chere: n., manner, 139; face, 857, entertainment, 747 (O.F. chere).
cherubinnes: n., of a cherub, 624 (O.E. cherubin, from Heb.).
chevisaunce: n., money lending, 282 (O.F. chevissance).
chiere: see **chere.**
chiknes: n., chickens, 380 (O.E. cicen).
chirche: n., church, 460 (O.E. cirice).
chivachye: n., mounted expedition, 85 (O.F. chivauche).
chivalrye: n., knightly conduct, 45 (O.F. chevalrie).
clad: v., see **clothe.**
clasp: v., buckle, 273 (Ety. dub.).
clause: n., sentence, a few words, 715 (Lat. clausam).
cleere: adv., clearly, 170 (O.F. cler + O.E. lic).
clene: adj., clean, pure, 504; adv., cleanly, 133 (O.E. clæne).
clennesse: n., purity, 506 (O.E. clænnes).
clense: v., purify, cleanse, 631 (O.E. clænsian).
clepen: v., call, 643 (O.E. cleopian).
clerk: n., student for Holy Orders, scholar, 285 (O.F. clerc).
cloke: n., cloak, 157 (O.F. cloque).
clooth: n., cloth, 447 (O.E. clap).
clothe: v., clothe, bind, cover. pp. clad, 103 (O.E. claoian).
cloysterer: n., one who lives in a cloister, a monk, 259 (O.F. cloister).
cloystre: n., cloister, 181 (O.F. cloistre).
cofre: n., chest, treasury, 298 (O.F. cofre).
cok: n., cook, 823 (O.E. cocc).
cold: n., cold, 420 (O.E. cald).
colerik: adj., choleric, see note to 587 (O.F. cholérique).
colpon: shred, bundle, hank, 679 (O.F. calpon).
comen: v., to come. Past sing., **cam,** 547; p.p., **come,** 23 (O.E. suman).
commissioun: n., royal warrant, 315 (Lat. commissionem).
companye: company, fellowship, 24, n. (O.F. conpaignie).
compeer: n., bosom friend, comrade, 670 (O.F. comper).
complexioun: n., temperament, 333. See note (Lat. complexionem).
composicioun: n., agreement, 848 (Lat. compositionem).
concubyn: n., light o' love, mistress, 650 (Lat. concubinam).
condicioun: n., state, rank in life, 38 (Lat. conditionem).
confort: n., pleasure, entertainment, 773 (O.F. confort).
connen: v., to know. Pres sing., **can;** past sing., **couthe, coude;** p.p. **couthe** (O.E. cunnan).
conscience: n., tender-heartedness, 142; conscientiousness, 398; conscience, 526 (Lat. conscientiam).
conseil: n., secret intention, 665; advice, 784 (O.F. conseil).
contree: n., country, district, 216 (O.F. contrée).
cop: n., top, 554 (O.E. cop).
cope: n., cape, 260 (Lat. capam).
coppe: n., cup, 134 (O.E. cuppa).
corage: n., heart, feeling, intent, disposition, -- (O.F. corage).
cordial: n., a heart stimulant, cordial, 443 (L.L. cordialem).
cosyn: n., related to, akin to, 742 (O.F. cosin).
cote: n., coat, 103 (O.F. cote).
coude: see **connen.**
countour: n., auditor, 359. See note (O.F. countour).
countrefete: v., imitate, 139 (Lat. contra + facio).
cours: n., course, 8 (O.F. cours).

courtepy: n., short coat, cape, 290 (M. Dutch, korte + pie).
couthe: see **connen.**
covenant: n., agreement, 600 (O.F. covenant).
coverchiefs: n., head coverings, kerchiefs, 453 (O.F. couvrechief).
cover: v., lay a table, 354 (O.F. couvrir).
covyne: n., trickery, deciet, 604 (O.F. couvine).
coy: adj., quiet, modest, shy, 119 (O.F. coi).
craft: adj., skill, 401; profession, 692 (O.E. cræft).
crie: v., cry out, shout, 636 (O.F. crier).
Cristen: adj., Christian, 55 (O.E. cristen).
Cristofre: n., a figure of St. Christopher, worn as a charm, 115. (Gk. X).
crop: n., new shoot, 7 (O.E. cropp).
crown: v., crown, surmount with a crown, 161 (O.F. coruner).
croys: n., cross, 699 (O.F. cross).
crulle: adj., curly, curled, 81 (O. Dutch, krull).
cryke: n., creek, inlet, 409 (O.F. crique).
curat: n., parish priest, 219 (L.L. curatus).
cure: n., care, attention, 303 (Lat. curam).
curious: adj., carefully made, beautiful, 196; expert, 577 (O.F. curius).
curs: n., excommunication, curse, 655 (Ety. dub.).
cursen: v., curse, excommunicate, 486 (Ety. dub.).
cursyng: n., excommunication, 660 (Ety. dub.).
curtesye: n., courtly behaviour, 46; politeness, 725 (O.F. cortesie).
curteys: adj., courteous, with courtly manners, 99; deferential, 250 (O.F. cort).
cut: n., lot, decisive choice, 835 (Welsh, cwt).

daliaunce: n., gossip, small talk, familiar conversation, 211 (O.F. daliaunce).
dauncen: v., dance, 96 (O.F. dancer).
daunce: n., dance. See note to 476 (O.F. dancer).
daunger: n., risk, 402; control, jurisdiction, 663 (O.F. dangier).
daungerous: adj., domineering, haughty, hard to please, awkward, 517 (O.F. dangeros).
dayerye: n., dairy, 597 (Cp. O.E. dæge, dairy-woman).
dayesye: n., daisy, 332 (O.E. dæges, eage).
decree: n., decree, document, 640 (O.F. decré).
dede: n., deed. **in deed;** indeed, 659 (O.E. dæd).
deed: adj., dead, 145 (O.E. dead).
deef: adj., deaf, 446 (O.E. deaf).
deel: n., share, part. **a great deel:** largely, to a great extent, 415 (O.F. dæl).
deelen: v., concern oneself with, be friendly with, 247 (O.E. dælan).
deeth: n., death, especially the Black Death, plague, 605 (O.E. dæp).
degree: n., rank, station of life, 40 (O.F. degre).
delve: v., dig, 536 (O.E. delfan).
delyt: n., delight, pleasure, 335 (O.F. delit).
delyvere: adj., active, sprightly, quick, 84 (O.F. delivre).
depe: adv., deeply, 129 (O.E. deope).
desdeyn: n., contempt, disdain, 789 (O.F. desdeigner).
despitous: adj., scornful, contemptuous, 516 (O.F. despire).
dette: n., debt, 280 (O.F. dete).
detteless: adj., free from debt, 582 (O.F. dete + O.E. læ).
devout: adj., pious, devout, 22 (O.F. devot).

devys: n., direction, decision, 816 (O.F. devis).
devyse: v., relate, describe, 34 (O.F. deviser).
deyntee: adj., rare, choice, 168; n., rarity, dainty, 346 (O.F. daintie).
deys: n., dais, platform, 370 (O.F. déys).
dide: see **doon.**
diete: n., diet, eating, 435 (O.F. diete).
digne: adj., worthy, 141; scornful, 517 (O.F. digne).
diligent: adj., painstaking, hard-working, 483 (O.F. diligent).
diocise: n., diocese, district, 664 (O.F. diocise).
dischevelee: adj., disheveled, with hair unkempt. 683 (O.F. deschevelé).
discreet: adj., tactful, discreet, 312 (O.F. discreet).
dispence: n., expenses, expenditure, 441 (O.F. dispens).
disport: n., cheerfulness, entertainment, diversion, 137 (O.F. desporter).
divyne: adj., divine, 122 (O.F. devin).
doctour: n., doctor, physician, 411 (O.F. doctour).
dokked: p.p., cut short, close cropped, 590 (Ety. dub.).
dong: n., dung, manure, 530 (O.F. dung).
doom: n., judgment, legal decision, 323 (O.E. dom).
doon: v., do, 78; **dooth:** pres. sing., 98; **doon:** pres. pl., 268; **dide:** past sing., 451 (O.E. don).
dore: door, 550 (O.E. duru).
dormant: adj., fixed, permanent. See note to 353 (O.F. dormir).
dorste: v., past sing. of **dar,** to dare, 227 (O.E. dorste).
doumb: adj., dumb, 774 (O.E. dumb).
doute: n., doubt, 487 (O.F. doute).
draughte: n., draught, drink, 135 (E.N.E., draft).
drawen: v., draw, 842; lead, 519; draweth, imp. pres., 835 (O.E. dragan).
drede: v., dread, fear exceedingly, 660 (O.E. drædan).
dresse: v., prepare, set in order, 106 (O.F. dresser).
drogges: n., drugs, medicines, 426 (O.F. drogue).
droghte: n., drought, 2 (O.E. drugoo).
drope: n., drop, 131 (O.E. dropa).
droupe: v., droop, 107. See note (O.N. drupa).
drye: adj., dry, 420. See note (O.E. dryge).
drynken: v., drink, 635; past pl., **dronken,** 820; p.p., **dronken,** 135 (O.E. drincen).
duzeyne: n., dozen, 578 (O.F. dozeine).
dyere: n., dyer, 362 (O.E. deag).
dyke: v., make ditches, 536 (O.E. dician).

ecclesiaste: n., preacher, 708 (O.F. ecclesiaste).
ech: addj., each, every, 39 (O.E. ælc).
echon: adj., pron., each one, 820 (O.E. ælc + an).
eek: adv., also, 5 (O.E. eac).
effect: n., reality, 319 (O.F. effect).
elles: adv., else, otherwise, 375 (O.E. elles).
embrounded: p.p., adorned, embroidered, 89 (O.F. embroder).
encombre: v., encumber, hamper, stick fast, 508 (O.F. encombrer).
encrees: n., increase, 275 (O.F. encreistre).
endite: v., compose, 95; draw up in legal form, 325 (O.F. enditer).
engendred: p.p., produced, generated, 4 (O.F. engendrer).
ensample: n., example, pattern, 496 (O.F. essample).
entuned: p.p., intoned, 123 (Lat. in + tonus).

envyned: p.p.p, supplied with wine, 342 (O.F. enviné).
er: adv., before, 36 (O.E. œr).
ercedeken: n., archdeacon, 655 (O.E. ærcediacon).
ere: n., ear. **eres:** pl., 556 (O.E. eare).
erly: adv., early, 33 (O.E. ærlice).
erst: adv., before, at first, 776 (O.E. ærest).
eschaunge: n., exchange. See note to 278 (O.F. eschange).
ese: n., ease, entertainment, comfort, 768 (O.F. aise).
esen: v., entertain, accommodate, 29 (O.F. aiser).
esily: adv., at her ease, 469 (O.F. aise + O.E. lice).
estaat, estat: n., condition, 203; rank, 522 (O.F. estat).
estatlich: adj., stately, 140 (O.F. estat + O.E. lic).
esy: adj., easy 223. See note to 441 (O.F. aisié).
even: adj., moderate, average, 83 (O.E. efen).
evermore: adv., always, 67 (O.E. æfre + mara).
everich: pron., every, each, 241 (O.E. æfre + ælc).
everichon: pron., every one, 31 (O.E. æfre + ælc + an).
everydeel: adv., entirely, 368 (O.E. æfre + ælc + dæl).
exemple: n., example, 568 (O.F. exemple).
eye: n., eye. Pl. **eyen,** 152. Sing., **ye,** 10 (O.E. eage).

facultee: n., profession, authority, position, 244 (Lat. facultatem).
fader, n., father, 100; gen. sing., 781 (O.E. fæder).
fair: adj., excellent, very good, 154; n., a good one, 165 (O.E. fæger).
faire: adv., excellently, gracefully, neatly, 94 (O.E. fægre).
fairnesse: n., beauty of example, integrity, goodness, 519 (O.E. fæger + nesse).
faldyng: n., coarse cloth, 391 (Ety. dub.).
fallen: v., fall, occur, happen; past sing. indic., **fil,** 845; past sing. subj., **fille,** 131; p.p., **falle,** 324 (O.E. feallan).
famulier: adj., on friendly terms, 215 (O.F. familier).
farsed: p.p., stuffed, crammed with, 233 (O.F. farcir).
faste: adv., close, near, 719 (O.E. fæste).
fayn: adv., gladly, 766 (O.E. fegn).
fee simple: n., unrestricted possession. (O.F. fee + simple).
feith: n., religion, faith, 62 (O.F. feid).
felawe: n., companion, comrade, 395 (O.N. felaga).
felawshipe: n., company, 26 (O.N. felaga + O.E. scipe).
felicitee: n., happiness, 338 (O.F. felicité).
fer: adv., far, 338; **ferre:** 48; **ferrer:** comp., 835; **ferreste:** superl., 494 (O.E. feorr, fierra, fierresta).
ferne: adj., ancient, distant, 14 (O.E. fyrn).
ferther: adv., further, 36 (O.E. furoor).
ferthing: n., a trace, 134; a small gift, 255 (O.E. feorthung).
festne: n., fasten, 195 (O.E. fæstnian).
fet: p.p., fetched, 819 (O.E. fetian).
fether: n., feather, 107 (O.E. feoer).
fetis: adj., elegant, neat, graceful, 157 (O.F. faitis).
fewe: adj., few, 639 (O.E. feawe).
feyne: v., pretend, feign, lie, 736 (O.F. feindre).
fiftene: adj., fifteen, 61 (O.F. fiftiene).
fighten: v., fight, p.p. foughten, 62 (O.E. feohtan).
figure: n., figure of speech, illustration, simile, 499 (Lat. figuram).

fil: see **fallen.**
first, firste: adv., first of all, 161 (O.E. fyrest).
firste: adj., first, 831 (O.E. fyrest).
fithele: n., fiddle, 296 (O.E. fioele).
flessh: n., flesh, meat, 147 (O.E. floesc).
flex: n., flex, 676 (O.E. fleax).
flour: n., flower, 4 (O.F. our).
flour-de-lys: n., lily-flower, 238 (O.F. flour + de + lis).
floytynge: adj., playing the flute, 91 (O.F. flauter).
folwen: v., follow; past sing., **folwed,** 528 (O.E. folgian).
fon: see **fynden.**
foo: n., fore, enemy, 63 (O.E. fah).
foot-mantel: see note to 472.
for: prep., since, seeing that, 443 (O.E. for).
foreward: n., agreement, promise, 33 (O.E. foreweard).
forheed: n., forehead, 154 (O.E. forheafod).
forme: n., ddue form, 305 (O.F. forme).
forneys: n., furance, 202 (O.F. fornais).
forpyned: adj., wasted by torture, 205 (O.E. for + pynian).
forster: n., forester, 117 (L.L. forestem).
fortunen: v., give good or bad fortune to. See note to 417 (O.F. fortuner).
foryeve: v., forgive, 743 (O.E. forgiefan).
fother: n., cart-load, 530 (O.E. fooer).
foul: adj., foul, impure, 501 (O.E. ful).
fowel: n., bird, 9 (O.E. fugol).
frankeleyn: n., a freeholder (O.F. fraunkeleyn).
fraternitee: n., guild, brotherhood, 364 (O.F. fraternité).
fredom: n., liberality, generosity, 46 (O.E. freodom).
freend: n., friend, 670 (O.E. freond).
frere: n., friar, 208 (O.F. frere).
fressh: adj., bright, fresh, 90; adv., 365 (O.E. fersc).
fro: prep., from, 44 (Icel. fra).
frye: v., fry, 383 (O.F. fryen).
ful: adj., full, 306; adv., very, 22 (O.E. ful).
fustian: n., coarse cloth, 75 (O.F. fustaigne).
fyn: adj., fine, 453 (O.F. fin).
fynch: n., finch. See note 652 (O.E. finc).
fry-reed: adj., as red as fire (O.E. fyr + read).

gadrede: past sing., gathered, 834 (O.E. gæderian).
gaf: see **yeve.**
galingale: n., the root of the sweet cyprus, 381 (O.F. galingal).
game: n., jest, 853; v., please, 534. See note (O.E. gamen).
gan: v., used to form past tense, with the sense of did. With participle to means began, past tense of **ginnen** (O.E. ginnan).
garleek: n., garlic, 634 (O.E. gar-leac).
gat: see **geten.**
gat-tothed: adj., see note to 468 (O.E. geat + too or O.E. gat + too).
gauded: p.p., with large beads, known as gauds (Lat. gaudia).
gay: adj., finely dressed, 74; handsome, 111; merry, 296 (O.F. gai).
geldyng: n., gelding, 691 (O.N. geldingr).
gentil: adj., of noble birth, 72; well-disposed, 567; comfortable, 718 (O.F. gentil).

gere: utensils, 352; clothing, 365 (O.E. gearwa).
gerland: n., garland, 666 (O.F. garlande).
gerner: n., garner, 593 (O.F. grenier).
gesse: v., suppose, think, imagine, 82 (Ety. dub.).
geten: v., obtain; past sing., **gat,** 703; p.p, **geten,** 291 (O.E. gietan).
gilty: adj., guilty, sinful, 660 (O.E. gyltig).
gipser: n., pouch, bag, 357 (O.F. gibecier).
girdel: n., girdle, belt, 358 (O.E. gyrdel).
girles: n., young people of both sexes, 664 (Ety. dub.).
girt: p.p., wearing a girdle, 329 (O.E. gyrdan).
glad: adj., happy, glad, 811 (O.E. glæd).
gladly: adv., gladly, readily, 308 (O.E. glæd + lice).
glarynge: adj., staring, 684 (O.E. glærgn).
glas: n., glass, mirror, 152 (O.E. glæs).
gobet: n,. piece, fragment, 696 (O.F. gobet).
goliardys: n., a buffoon, foul-mouthed jester, 560 (O.F. gouliardois).
gonne: see **gan.**
good: adj., good, 183.
good: n., goods, property, 581 (O.E. god).
goon, go: v., go, 12; pres. pl., **goon,** 769; p.p. **y-go,** 286 (O.E. gan).
goost: n., ghost, 205 (O.E. gast).
goot: n., goat, 688 (O.E. gat).
gospel: n., gospel, 481 (O.E. god + spel).
governaunce: n., control, management, 281 (O.F. gouvernance).
governour: n., umpire, 813; governor, controller, 861 (O.F. gouvernour).
governyng: n., control, management, 599 (O.F. gouverner).
gowne: n., gown, 391 (O.F. goune).
grace: n., favour, 88 (O.F. grace).
graunten: v., agree to; past pl. 768 (O.F. granter).
grey: adj., gray, 152. See note (O.E. græg).
grece: n., grease, 135 (O.F. gresse).
greet: adj., great, 84; n., a great one, 339; **gretter,** comp.; **greteste,** super., 120 (O.E. great).
grehoundes: n., greyhounds, 190 (O.E. grihund).
grene: adj., green, 607; n., 103 (O.E. grene).
greyn: n., grain, 596 (O.F. grain).
grope: v., test, search deeply, 644 (O.E. grapian).
ground: n., texture, 453 (O.E. grund).
ground: v., instruct, 414 (O.E. grund).
grys: n., gray fur, possibly of squirrel, 194 (O.F. gris).
gyde: n., guide, leader, 804 (O.F. guider).
gynglen: v., jingle, 170 (Echoic in origin).
gypoun: n, tunic, short vest, 75 (O.F. jupon).
gyse: n., fashion, 663 (O.F. guise).

haberdasher: n., a dealer in small wares, haberdasher, 361 (A.F. hapertas).
habergeoun: n., a coat of mail, habergeon, hauberk, 76 (O.F. haubejon).
half: adj., half, 8 (O.E. healf).
halle: n., hall, living room, 353 (O.E. heall).
halwe: n., shrine, saint, 14 (O.E. halga).
han: see **haven.**
hangen: v., to hang; past sing., **heng,** 160, **heeng,** 358; past pl., **henge,** 677 (O.E. hangian).

happe: v., happen, befall, 585 (O.N. happ).
hardily: adv., boldly, certainly, surely, 156 (O.F. harai + O.E. lice).
hardy: adj., hold, courageous, 405 (O.F. hardi).
hare: n., hare, 191 (O.E. hara).
harlot: n., fellow rascal (O.F. harlot).
harlotrye: n., unseemly jests, scurrilous tales, 561 (O.F. harlot + rie).
harm: n., matter for regret, pity, 385 (O.E. hearm).
harneysed: p.p., mounted, ornamented, 114 (O.F. harnaschier).
harpyng: n., playing on the harp, 266 (O.E. hearpian).
harre: n., hinge, hinges, 550 (O.E. heorr).
haten: v., to be called; past sing., **highte,** 616 (O.E. hatan).
haunt: n., practice, skill habit, 447 (O.F. hanter).
haven: v., have; 3rd pres. sin., **hath,** 2; pres. pl., **han,** 849; past sing., **hadde,** 31; **hade,** 554 (O.E. habban).
haven: n., harbour, 407 (O.E. hæfen).
heed: n., head, 198 (O.E. heafod).
heede: n., heed, care, attention, 198 (O.E. hedan).
heeld: see **holden.**
heeng: see **hangen.**
heep: n., crowd, number, 575 (O.E. heap).
heer: n., hair, 589; pl. **herys,** 555 (O.E. hær).
heeth: n., heath, 6 (O.E. hæþ).
heere: v., hear, 175; past sing., **herde,** 221; p.p., **herd,** 849 (O.E. hieran).
heigh: adj., high, 316 (O.E. heah).
helle: n., hell, 658 (O.E. hell).
helpen: v., to help, 258; **helpen of:** cure, 632; p.p. **holpen,** 18 (O.E. helpan).
hem: pron., them, 11 (O.E. heom).
heng: v., see **hangen.**
henten: v., seize, catch, 299.
herberwe: n., harbour, 403; inn, 765 (O.E. hentan).
herde: n., shepherd, herdsman, 603 (O.E. hierde).
herde: v., see **heere.**
here: n., see **heer.**
herknen: v., listen; imperative pl., **herkneth,** 788 (O.E. hercnian).
herte: n., heart, 150 (O.E. heorte).
herys: n., see **beer.**
hertely: adv., cordially, sincerely, 762 (O.E. heorte + lice).
hethen: n., heathen, 66 (O.E. hæoen).
hethenesse: n., heathendom, 49 (O.E. hæden + nesse).
heven: n., heaven, 519 (O.E. heofon).
heven: v., heave, lift, 550 (O.E. hebban).
hewe: n., complexion, colour, 394 (O.E. hiew).
hider: adv., hither, 672 (O.E. hider).
highte: see **haten.**
him: pron., him (O.E. him).
himself: pron., himself, 219 (O.E. him + selfan).
himselven: see **himself.**
hipe: n., hip, 472 (O.E. hype).
hir: adj., their (O.E. hiera).
hir: pron., her (O.E. hiere).
his: adj., his (O.E. his).
holden: v., consider, keep, hold; past sing., **heeld,** 176; impera. pres., **hoold,** 783; p.p., **holden,** 141 (O.E. healdan).
holpen: see **helpen.**

holpen: see **helpen.**
holt: n., wood, copse, 6 (O.E. holt).
holwe: adj., hollow, empty, 289 (O.E. holb).
homward: adv., on the way home, 794 (O.E. ham + weard).
hond: n., hand, 193 (O.E. hond).
honeste: adj., honourable, respectable, 246 (O.F. honeste).
honour: n., honourable conduct, 46 (O.F. onor).
hood: n., hood, 680 (O.E. hod).
hool: adj., whole, 533 (O.E. hal).
hoolly: adv., completely, wholly, 599 (O.E. hal + lice).
hooly: adj., holy, 17 (O.E. halig).
hoom: adv., home, 400 (O.E. ham).
hoomly: adv., in a plain, homely manner, 328 (O.E. ham + lice).
hoost: n., inn-keeper, host, 747 (O.F. hoste).
hoot: adj., hot, fervent, 394 (O.E. hat).
hoote: adv., hotly fervently, ardently, 97 (O.E. hate).
hors: n., horse, horses, 74, 598 (O.E. hors).
hosen: n., stockings, 456 (O.E. hosan).
hostelrye: n., inn, hostelry, 23 (O.F. hostel + rie).
hostiler: n., inn-keeper, 241 (O.F. hostel + er).
hound: n., hound dog, 146 (O.E. hund).
houre: n., an astrological hour, 416 (O.F. ure).
hous: n., convent, monastery, 252; house, mansion, 343 (O.E. hus).
housbond: n., husband, 460 (O.E. hus + bond).
housholdere: n., head of a household, 339 (O.E. hus + heald + ere).
humour: n., humour (O.F. humor).
hy: adj., high, lofty, 306; comp., **hyer,** 399 (O.E. heah).
hye: adv., high, aloft, 271 (O.E. heahe).
hyndreste: adj., hindmost, last, 622 (O.E. hinder + este).
hyne: n., farm-servant, 603 (O.E. hine).
hyre: n., hire, rent, 507 (O.E. hyr).

i-drawe: v., see **drawen.**
ilke: adj., same, 64 (O.E. ilca).
infect: adj., invalidated, proved illegal, 320 (Lat. infectum).
inne: prep., in, 41 (O.E. inne).
inspire: v., to animate, quicken, 6 (Lat. inspiro).
iren: n., iron, 500 (O.E. iren).

janglere: n., noisy fellow, loud talker, 560 (O.F. janglere).
jape: n., jest, trick, 705 (Ety. dub.).
jay: n., jay, a bird, 642 (O.F. jay).
jet: n., fashion, style, 682 (O.F. jet).
jolitee: n., bravado, fun, 680 (O.F. jolif + tie).
juge: n., judge, umpire, 814 (O.F. juge).
juggement: n., opinion, decision, 778 (O.F. jugement).
justen: v., joust, tilt in the lists, 96 (O.F. juster).
justice: n., judge, 314 (O.F. justise).

keep: n., heed, care, attention, 398 (O.E. cep(an)).
kene: adj., keen, sharp, 104 (O.E. cene).
kepe: v., keep, take heed, 130; past sing., **kepte,** 512; take care of, 415; guarded, 276 (O.E. cepan).

kepere: n., keeper, prior, 172 (O.E. cep + er).
kerven: v., carve; past sing., **carf,** 100 (O.E. ceorfan).
knarre: n., thick-set fellow, 549 (Ety. dub.).
knobbe: n., knob, 633 (Ety. dub.).
knowen: v., know, 382; pres. pl., **knowen,** 642; past sing., **knew,** 240 (O.E. cnawan).
knyf: n., knife, 233 (O.E. cnif).
kynde: adj., kindly, 647 (O.E. cynde).

laas: n., cord, lace, string, 392 (O.F. laz).
labouren: v., toil, 186 (O.F. labourer).
lady: n., lady. See note to line 88 (O.E. hlæfdige).
lafte: see **leven.**
lakken: v., be lacking to, 756 (O.N. lakv).
langage: n., language, words, 211 (O.F. langage).
lappe: n., lap, 686 (O.E. læppa).
large: adj., large, broad, 472 (O.F. large).
large: adv., freely, 734 (O.F. large).
late: adv., recently, 77 (O.E. late).
latoun: n., latten, 699. See note (O.F. laton).
lay: see **liggen.**
lazar: n., leper, 242 (L.L. lazarus).
lecherous: adj., lustful, wanton, 626 (O.F. lecheros).
leed: n., leaden cauldron, 202 (O.E. lead).
leef: adj., lief, pleasant, welcome; comp., **levere,** 193 (O.E. leof).
leene: adj., lean, 591; thin (O.E. hlæne).
legge: n., leg, 591 (O.N. leggr).
lekes: n., leeks, 634 (O.E. leac).
lenen: v., lend, 611 (O.E. lænan).
lenger: see **long.**
lengthe: n., height, length, 83 (O.E. lengou).
lernen: v., learn, 308; p.p., **lerned,** 613 (O.E. leornian).
lernynge: n., instruction, 300 (O.E. leornung).
lessoun: n., lesson as read in church, 709. See note (O.F. leçon).
lest: n., pleasure, desire, delight, 132 (O.E. lyste).
leste: see **listen.**
leten: v., let, allow, permit, abandon; past sing., **leet,** 128; impera., **lat,** 188; **lat be,** put aside, 840; **lat se,** let use see, 831 (O.E. lætan).
letuaries: n., remedies, powders mixed with honey, 426 (O.F. letuaire).
leven: v., cease; past sing., **lafte,** 492 (O.E. læfan).
levere: see **leef.**
lewed: adj., ignorant of book learning, uneducated, 502 (O.E. læwede).
leyen: v., lay, place; p.p., **leyd,** 81 (O.E. lecgan).
licentiat: n., a friar holding a licence from the pope to hear confessions, licentiate, 220 (L.L. licentiatum).
licour: n., sap, 3 (O.F. licour).
liggen: v., lie, lodge; past sing., **lay,** 20 (O.E. licgan).
liketh: v., impers, it pleases you, 777 (O.E. lician).
liknen: v., resemble, 180.
limitour: n., limitor (O.F. limiteur).
lippe: n., lip, 128 (O.E. lippa).
lipsen: v., lisp, 264 (O.E. wlispian).
listen: v., impers., it pleases; past sing., **liste,** 102, **leste,** 750 (O.E. lystan).
listes: n., the lists at a tournament, 63 (O.E. liste).

litarge: n., litharge, ointment made from lead oxide, 629 (O.F. litarge).
lite: adj., little, small, 494 (O.E. lyt).
litel: adj., little, 87 (O.E. lytel).
liven: v., live, 506; **livynge:** pres. part., 532 (O.E. libban).
liveree: n., livery of a guild, uniform, habit, 363 (O.F. livrée).
lodemenage: n., steersmanship, skill as a pilot, 403 (O.E. lad + O.F. menage).
logik: n., logic, 286 (L.L. logicam).
lokkes: n., locks, curls, 81 (O.E. locc).
lond: n., land, 14; **upon lond:** in the country, 702 (O.E. lond).
long: adj., long, 354; comp., **lenger,** 330 (D.E. long).
longen: v., desire greatly, yearn, 12 (O.E. longian).
looken: v., look, seem, 289 (O.E. locian).
looth: adj., unwilling, reluctant, 486 (O.E. lao).
lord: n., lord, master, 47 (O.E. hlaford).
lordynges: n., sirs, my masters, 761 (O.E. hlaford + ing).
lore: n., teaching, doctrine, learning, 527 (O.E. lar).
loude: adv., loudly, 171 (O.E. hlude).
love: n., love, 475; sweetheart, 672 (O.E. lufu).
lovedayes: n., lovedays. See note to 258 (O.E. lufu + dæg).
loveknotte: n., love-knot, 196 (O.E. lufu + cnotta).
lovyere: n., lover, 80 (O.E. lufian + er).
lowe: adj., low, 522 (O.N. lagr).
lowly: adj., humble, 99 (O.N. lagr + O.E. lice).
luce: n., pike, 350 (O.F. lus).
lust: n., delight, pleasure, 192 (O.E. lust).
lusty: adj., merry, joyful, gay, 80 (O.E. lust + y).
lye: v., tell falsehoods, lie, 659 (O.E. leogan).
lyf: n., life, 71 (O.E. lif).
lyk: adj., like, 259 (O.E. lic).
lynen: v., to line, 440 (O.E. linen).
lyve: n., life, (O.E. lif).

maad: v., see **maken.**
madame: n., my lady, madame, 121 (O.F. ma + dame).
made: v., see **maken.**
magik: n., magic. See note to 416 (Lat. artem magicam).
maister, maistre: n., master, one in authority, 261 (O.F. maistre).
maistrye: n., superiority, excellence, authority. See note on 165 (O.F. maistrie).
maken: v., make, cause, 184; compose, draw up, 325; past tense, **made** or **maked;** p.p., **maad,** 212 (O.E. macian).
maladye: n., ailment, malady, 419 (O.F. maladie).
male: n., wallet, bag, 694 (O.F. male).
man: n., man, 167; as indef. pronoun, as a means of forming passive, 149, etc. (O.E. man).
maner: n., sort, kind, 71 (O.F. manière).
manhod: n., manhood, manliness, 756 (O.E. man + had).
manly: adj., manly. See note to 167 (O.E. man + ly).
mantel: n., cloak, 378 (O.F. mantel).
marchal: n., master of the ceremonies, steward, 752 (O.F. mareschal).
marchant: n., merchant, 270 (O.F. marchant).
mariage: n., marriage, wedding, 212 (O.F. mariage).

martir: n., martyr, 17 (O.E. martyr).
marybones: n., marrow-bones, 380 (O.E. mearg + ban).
matere: n., matter, business, 727 (O.F. matière).
maunciple: n., manciple (O.F. mancipe).
may: v., may. See **mowen.**
mayde: n., maid, girl, 69 (O.F. mægden).
mede: n., reward, 770 (O.E. med).
medlee: n., see note to 328 (O.F. medle).
meede: n., meadow, 89 (O.E. mæd).
meeke: adj., modest, 69 (O.F. meoc).
melodye: n., melody, song, 9 (O.F. melodie).
men: pron., one. Used to make passive voice. **See man.**
mene: v., mean, 793 (O.E. mænan).
mercenarie: n., hireling, 514 (Lat. mercenarium).
mere: n., mare, 541 (O.E. mere).
merye, mery, mury, myrie: adj., merry, 208, 757, 802 (O.E. myrge).
meschef: n., mischief, misfortune, 493 (O.F. meschief).
mesurable: adj., moderate, temperate, 435 (O.F. mesurable).
mete: n., food, 136; mealtime, 127 (O.E. mete).
mewe: n., coop, 349 (O.F. mue).
might: n., power, 538 (O.E. miht).
mighte: v., see **mowen.**
mighty: adj., strong, powerful, 108 (O.E. mihtig).
milk: n., milk, 147 (O.E. meolc).
millere: n., miller, 542 (O.E. mylen + er).
miscarie: v., come to harm, 513 (O.E. mis + O.F. carier).
mister: n., craft, trade, 613 (O.F. mester).
mo: adv., more, 576 (O.E. ma).
moneye: n., money, 703 (O.F. moneye).
monk: n., monk, member of a monastic order, 165 (O.E. munuc).
month: n., month, 92 (O.E. monao).
moo: adj., more, 101 (O.E. ma).
moone: n., moon, 403 (O.E. mona).
moore: adv., in greater measure, to a greater degree, 219 (O.E. mara).
moost: adv., especially, in very large measure, 561 (O.E. mæst).
moot, moote, mote: v., must, ought, 232 742, 832; **moste:** had to, 712 (O.E. mot).
moral: adj., moral, godly, 307 (Lat. moralem).
mormal: n., inflamed sore, 386 (O.F. mortmal).
morne: n., morning, 358 (O.E. morgen).
morsel: n., portion, fragment (O.F. morsel).
mortal: adj., deadly, 61 (O.F. mortel).
mortreux: n., see note to 384 (O.F. mortreux).
morwe: n., morning, 334 (O.E. morgen).
moste: v., see **moot.**
mote: v., see **moot.**
motteley: n., striped clothing (Ety. dub.).
mous: n., mouse, 144 (O.E. mus).
mouth: n., mouth, 153 (O.E. muþ).
mowen: v., be able; pres. sing., **may,** 737; past sing., **mighte,** 169 (O.E. mæg).
moyste: adj., soft, pliable, 457; n., moisture, 420 (O.F. moiste).
muche: adj., great, 494 (O.E. mycel).
muchel: adv., greatly, a great deal, 258 (O.E. mycel).
muchel: n., a great amount, 211 (O.E. mycel).

mury: adj., see **merye.**
murierly: adv., the more merrily, 714 (O.E. myrig + er + lice).
myn: adj., my, mine, 804 (O.E. min).
myre: n., mire, 508 (O.N. myrr).
myrie: adj., see **merye.**
myrthe: n., amusement, merriment, jest, 759 (O.E. myrigo).
myselven: pron., myself, 803 (O.E. me + self).

nacion: n., nation, 53 (O.F. nacioun).
namo: adj., no more, 544 (O.E. na + ma).
naretten: v., see **aretten.**
narwe: adj., narrow, close together, 625 (O.E. nearu).
nas: v., see **been.**
nat: adv., not, 74 (O.E. naht).
nathelees: adv., nevertheless, none the less, 35 (O.E. na + þe + læs).
natureel: adj., natural. See note on 416 (O.F. natural).
nature: n., nature, disposition, kind, 11 (O.F. nature).
naught: pron., 756 (O.E. na + wiht).
ne: adv., nor, 603 (O.E. ne).
neden: v., be necessary; pres. sing., 462 (O.E. neodian).
neede: adj., necessary, 304 (O.E. niede).
neer: adv., nearer, 839 (O.E. near).
neet: n., cattle, 597 (O.E. neat).
neighebour: n., neighbour, 535 (O.E. neahgebur).
nekke: n., neck, 238 (O.E. knecca).
never, nevere: adv., never, 70 (O.E. næfre).
newe: adj., new, fashionable, modern, 176; adv., newly recently, 365 (O.E. newe).
nightertale: n., night-time, 97 (O.E. niht + getal).
nightyngale: n., nightingale, 98 (O.E. nihtegale).
noble: adj., notable, distinguished, noble, 60 (O.F. noble).
noght: adv., not at all, by no means, 107 (O.E. naht).
nolde: v., see **shal.**
nombre: n., number, 716 (O.F. nombre).
nones: n., occasion, time. See note to 379 (O.F. þa)n + anes).
nonne: n., nun, 118 (O.E. nunne).
noon: pron. and adj., none, no one, 210 (O.E. nan).
noot: v., see **wite.**
norissyng: n., nourishment, 437 (O.F. noriss + O.E. yng).
nose: n., nose, 123 (O.E. nosu).
nosethirles: n., nostrils, 557 (O.E. nosu + ovrel).
note: n., tune, note, 235 (O.F. nota).
not-heed: n., closely cropped head, 109 (O.E. knot + heafod).
nowthe: adv., now, at the moment, 462 (O.E. nu + þa).
now: adv., now, 715 (O.E. nu).
nowher: adv., nowhere, 251 (O.E. na + hwær).
ny: adv., closely, 588 (O.E. neah).
nyce: adj., fastidious, scrupulous, 398 (O.F. nice).
nyne: adj., nine, 24 (O.E. nigon).

o: adj., one, 304 (O.E. a).
obstinat: adj., obstinate, 521 (Lat. obstinatus).
of: prep., of, about, within, 87; some, 146 (O.E. of).

offertorie: n., see note to 710 (Lat. offertorium).
office: n., secular employment: 292 (O.F. office).
offrynge: n., offering (O.E. offrung).
ofte: adj., many, 485 (O.E. oft).
oftetyme: adv., often, 52 (O.E. oft + tima).
oghte: v., see **owen.**
old: adj., old (O.E. eald).
ones: one and the same time, 765 (O.E. anes).
oon: adj., one, the same (O.E. an).
ooth: n., oath, 120 (O.E.).
open: adj., open, 10 (O.E. open).
opinioun: n., opinion, 183 (O.F. opinion).
ordre: n., monastic order, order of friars, 214 (O.F. ordre).
other: adj., other, 113 (O.E. ooer).
othes: n., see **ooth.**
ounce: n., small piece, bunch, 677 (O.F. once).
oure: pron. and adj., our, 34 (O.F. eower).
out. adv., out, 45 (O.E. ut).
outrely: adv., entirely, utterly, without gainsaying, 237 (O.E. uterlice).
outrydene: n., rider out. See note to 166 (O.E. ut + ridan + er).
overest: adj., upper, uppermost, topmost, 290 (O.E. ofer).
overal: adv., everywhere, wherever, 216 (O.E. ofer + eall).
overlippe: n., top lip, upper lip, 133 (O.E. ofer + lippa).
oversprede: v., spread over; past tense, **overspradde,** 678 (O.E. over + sprædan).
owen: v., owe., own; past tense, **oghte,** 505, ought (O.E. agan).
owher: adv., anywhere, 653 (O.E. a + hwær).
owne: adj., own, 213 (O.E. agen).
oynement: n., ointment, 631 (O.F. oignement).
oynon: n., onion, 634 (O.F. oynoun).
oystre: n., oyster, 182 (O.F. oistre).

paas: n., pace, walking pace, 825 (O.E. pas).
pace: v., go, pass, outstrip, 36 (O.F. passer).
pacient: n., patient, 484 (Lat. patientem).
pale: adj., pale, 205 (O.E. pale).
palfrey: n., palfrey, saddle-horse, 207 (O.F. palefrei).
palmere: n., palmer (O.F. palmer).
pardee: anteri., By God, 563 (O.F. par + dé).
pardoner: n., pardoner (O.F. pardun + er).
pardon: n., pardon, indulgence, 687 (O.F. pardun).
parfit: adj., perfect, 72 (O.F. parfit).
parisshe: n., parish, 449 (O.F. paroche).
parisshen: n., parishoner, 482 (O.F. paroissen).
partrich: n., partridge, 349 (O.F. perdriz).
parvys: n., church porch. See note to 310 (O.F. parevis).
passen: v., pass, surpass, cross, 448 (O.F. passer).
patente: n., patent (Lat. patenten).
paye: v., pay, 539 (O.F. payer).
pecok; n., peacock, 104 (O.E. pea + coc).
pees: n., peace, 532 (O.F. pais).
peire: n., set, string, rosary, 159 (O.F. paire).
penaunce: n., penance, 223 (O.F. peneance).

peple: n., people, 700 (O.F. people).
perce: v., pierce, 2 (O.F. percer).
perchaunce: adc., indeed, perhaps, 475 (O.F. per + chance).
pers: adj., bluish-grey, 439 (O.F. pers).
person, persone, persoun: n., parson, parish priest, 478; person, 521 (O.F. persone).
pestilence: n., plague time, epidemic, 442 (Lat. pestilentiam).
peynen: v., take pains, endeavour, 139 (O.F. peyne + en).
philosophre: n., philosopher, alchemist, 297. See note (O.F. philosophe).
philosophye: n., philosophy, 295 (Lat. philosophiam).
phisyk: n., medicine, 411 (L.L. physician).
pigges: n., gen. pl., pigs, 700 (?O.E. picga).
piled: adj., deprived of, plucked, scanty, 627 (O.F. piller).
pilwe-beer: n., pillow case, 694 (O.E. pyle — bær).
pin: n., pin, 234 (O.E. pinn).
pinchen: v., cavil at, 326; pleat, 151 (O.F. pincer).
pitaunce: n., portion of food, 224 (O.F. pitance).
pitous: adj., compassionate, full of pity, 143 (O.F. pitous).
plentevous: adj., abundant, plenteous, 344 (O.F. plentivous).
plesaunt: adj., pleasing, agreebale, 138 (O.F. plaisant).
plesen: v., please, 610 (O.F. plaisir).
pleyen: v., play, amuse oneself, jest, 236 (O.E. plegean).
pleyn: adj., absolute, full, 315; adv., fully, 327 (O.F. plain).
pleyn: adv., plainly, 790 (O.F. plain).
pleynly: adv., openly, 727 (O.F. plain + ly).
plowman: n., ploughman, small farmer, 529 (O.E. plog + mann).
point: n., point, 114; condition, 200 (O.F. point).
pomely: adj., dappled, 616 (O.F. pommele).
pompe: n., ostentation, display, 525 (Lat. pompam).
pope: n., pope, person of authority, 261 (O.E. papa).
poraille: n., poor people, rabble, 247 (O.F. poverail).
port: n., bearing, manner, demeanour, 69 (O.F. port).
post: n., pillar, support, 214 (O.E. post).
pouch: n., pouch, purse, 368 (O.F. poche).
poudre: n., powder, 381 (O.F. poudre).
poudre-marchant: n., flavouring powder, 381 (O.F. poudre + marcheante).
pouren: v., pore over, study closely, 185 (Ety. dub.).
povre: adj., poor, 225 (O.F. poore).
power: n., power, authority, 218 (O.F. pooir).
poynaunt: adj., pungent, piquant, highly flavoured, 352 (O.F. poignant).
poynt: n., condition, 200 (O.F. poynt).
practisour: n., practitioner, 422 (O.F. pratiser).
prechen: v., preach, 481 (O.F. prechier).
preest: n., priest, 164 (O.E. preost).
prelaat: n., prelate, ecclesiastic, 204 (O.F. prélat).
press: n., press, mould, machine, 81 (O.F. presse).
preyen: v., pray, 301 (O.F. preier).
preyere: n., prayer, 231 (O.F. preiere).
prikasour: n., hard rider (O.E. prician).
priken: v., spur, incite, 11 (O.E. prician).
prikyng: n., tracking a hare by its footprints (O.E. pricung).
prioresse: n., prioress, head of a convent (O.F. prioresse).
prively: adv., secretly, 609 (O.F. privé + ly).
profit: n., advantage, profit, 249 (O.F. profit).

propre: adj., own, 540 (O.F. propre).
proprely: adv., exactly, accurately, 729 (O.F. propre + ly).
proven: v., prove true, stood the test of experience, 547 (O.F. prover).
prys: n., reputation, renown, esteem, price, prize, 67 (O.F. prys).
pullen: v., pull (O.E. pullian).
pultrye: n., poultry, 598 (O.F. pultrie).
punysshe: v., punish, 657 (O.F. punir).
purchacen: v., buy, 608 (O.F. purchacer).
purchas: n., see note to 256.
purchasour: n., buyer up of land, 318 (O.F. purchaseur).
purchasyng: n., transaction of buying up land, 320 (O.F. purchas + O.E. yng).
purfile: v., trim, edge, 193 (O.F. pourfiler).
purs: n., money bag, purse, 656 (O.E. purs).
purtreye: v., draw, portray, 96 (O.F. portraire).
pye: n., pie, 384 (Ety. dub.).

quik: adj., lively, animated, 306 (O.E. cwic).
quod: v., said, 839 (O.E. cwæp).
quiksilver: n., mercury, 629 (O.E. cwic + seolfor).
quyte: v., reward, pay, repay, 770 (O.F. quiter).

rage: v., behave noisily, romp, 257 (O.F. ragier).
rake: n., rake, 287 (O.E. raca).
ram: n., sign Aries in the Zodiac, 8; prize for wrestling, 548 (O.E. ramm).
rather: adv., by preference, sooner, 487 (O.E. haaoer).
raughte: v., see **rechen.**
rebel: adj., rebellious, 833 (O.F. rebelle).
rechen: v., reach out; past tense, **raughte,** 136 (O.E. ræcan).
recchelees: adj., negligent, careless, 179 (O.E. receleas).
recorde: v., recall, bring to memory, 829 (O.F. recorder).
reden: v., advise, 741; read, 709 (O.E. rædan).
redy: adj., ready, prepared, 21 (O.E. ræde).
reed: n., adviser, counsellor, 665 (O.E. ræd).
reed: adj., red, 90 (O.E. read).
reherce: v., rehearse, relate, 732 (O.F. rehercier).
rekene: v., reckon, calculate, 401 (O.E. recenian).
rekenyng: account, 600 (O.E. recenung).
religioun: n., religion, 477 (O.F. religion).
relik: n., relic, 701 (O.F. relique).
remedyes: n., potions, charms, 475 (O.F. remedie).
remenaunt: n., remainder, 724 (O.F. remenant).
rennen: v., run; past tense, **ran,** 509 (O.E. rinnan).
rennyng: n., running, 551 (O.N. renna + O.E. ung).
renoun: n., reputation, 316 (O.F. renoun).
rente: n., income (O.F. rente).
repentaunt: adj., repentant, contrite, penitent, 228 (O.F. repentant).
reportour: n., umpire, judge, 814 (O.F. reporteur).
reserve: v., reserve, keep, 188 (O.F. reserver).
reson: n., opinion, reason, common sense, 37 (O.F. resoun).
reste: n., rest, bed, 30 (O.E. ræst).
reule: n., monastic, discipline, rule, 173 (O.F. riule).
reule: v., rule, control, guide, 816 (O.F. riuler).

reve: n., reeve (O.E. refa).
reverence: n., honour, reverence, respect, respectful manner, 141 (Lat. reverentiam).
reyn: n., rain, 492 (O.E. regn).
reyse: v., go on a military expedition, see service, 54 (O.E. ræsan).
riche: adj., rich, 311; rich people, 248 (O.F. riche).
right: adv., exactly, very, 257 (O.E. rihte).
robes: n., robe, 296 (O.F. robe).
roialliche: adv., in a regal manner, as would become a princess, 378 (O.F. roial + O.E. lice).
rood: v., see **ryden.**
roos: v., see **rysen.**
roost: n., roast meat, 206 (O.F. rost).
roste: v., to roast, 383; pp., **rosted,** 147 (O.F. rostir).
rote: n., root, 2 (O.N. rot).
rote: n., a small harp, 236 (O.F. rote).
rote: n., rote, heart, 327 (O.F. rote).
rouncy: n., a hack, nag, a poor sort of horse, 390 (O.F. ronoin).
round: adv., round, 589 (O.F. roond).
rounded: v., took a round form, 263 (O.F. rondir).
route: n., company, 622 (O.F. route).
rudeliche: adv., roughly, rudely, broadly, 734 (O.F. ruide + O.E. lice).
ruste: v., grew rusty, deteriorate, 502 (O.E. rustian).
rusty: adj., rusty, 618 (O.E. rustig).
ryde: v., ride; past sing.,**rood,** 169; past pl., **riden,** 825.
ryse: v., rise; past sing., **roos,** 823.

sake: n., sake, 537 (O.E. sacu).
sangwyn: adj., blood-red, 333; n., stuff of a blood-red colour, 439 (O.F. sanguine).
saugh: v., see **seen.**
sautrie: n., psaltery, 296 (O.F. sautier).
save: prep., except, 683 (O.F. sauf).
save: v., save from penalty, 661 (O.F. salver).
sawcefleem: adj., pimpled, 625 (O.F. sauce + fleume).
scalled: adj., scabby, scurfy, 627 (O.E. sceallu).
scarsly: adv., frugally, sparely, 583 (O.F. escars).
scathe: n., harm, misfortune, pity, 466 (O.N. skadi).
science: n., knowledge, 316 (Lat. scientiam).
sclendre: adj., slight, 587 (O.F. esclendre).
scole: n., school, 125 (O.E. scoler).
scoler: n., student, 260 (O.E. scolere).
scoleye: v., to attend the university school, study, 302 (O.F. secoleier).
seche: v., seek, 13 (O.E. secen).
see: n., sea, 59 (O.E. sæ).
seege: n., siege, 56 (O.F. siege).
seek: adj., sick, ill, 18; sike, 245 (O.E. seoc).
seen: v., see; past sing., **saugh,** 144; **seigh,** 193 (O.E. seon).
seigh: v., see **seen.**
seken: v., see **seche.**
selle: v., barter, exchange, 278 (O.E. sellan).
selleres: n., sellers, 248 (O.E. sellere).
semen: v., seem, 39 (O.E. seman); **semely:** adj.; suitable, 751 (O.N. sæmiligr).

semely: adv., seemly, suitably, becomingly, 123 (O.N. semiliga).
semycope: n., short cape, 262 (Lat. semi + L.L. capa).
sendal: n., a fine silk, 440 (O.F. sendal).
senden: v., send, 426 (O.E. sendan).
sene: adj., visible, 134 (O.E. siene).
sentence: n., import, meaning, 306 (O.F. sentence).
sergeaunt: n., sergeant. See note to 309 (O.F. serjant).
servant: n., retainer, 101 (O.F. servant).
serve: v., serve, profit, 187 (O.F. servir).
servysable: adj., anxious to serve, 99 (O.F. servisable).
service, servyce: service, 250; liturgy, 122 (O.F. servise).
seson: n., season, 19 (O.F. saison).
sessiouns: n., sessions of the law-courts, 355 (O.F. session).
sethe: v., seethe, boil, 383 (O.E. seooan).
sette: v., place, arrange, set, 815 (O.E. settan).
seye, seyn: v. say, 181; pres. sing., **seith,** 178; past sing., **sayde,** 70 (O.E. secgan).
seyl: n., sail, 696 (O.E. segl).
shadwen: V., shade, 607 (O.E. sceadwian).
shal: v., must, shall, 853; past tense, **sholde,** 184 (O.E. scal).
seyl: n., sail, 696 (O.E. segl).
shame: n., disgrace, 503 (O.E. scamu).
shamefastness: n., shyness, modesty, 840 (O.E. scantfæst + nesse).
shapen: v., prepare, intend, 772 (O.E. sceapan).
shaply: adj., fit, 372 (O.E. sceap + lic).
sharply: adv., severely, 523 (O.E. scearp + lice).
shave: v., shave, 588 (O.E. sceafan).
sheef: n., sheaf, 104 (O.E. sceaf).
sheeld: n., a French coin, écu, 278 (O.E. scield).
shene: adj., bright, beautiful, 115 (O.E. sciene).
sheren: v., cut, shear, 589 (O.E. sciran).
shinne: n., shin, 386 (O.E. scinu).
shipman: n., sailor, 388 (O.E. scipu + mann).
shire: n., county, shire, 15 (O.E. scir).
shirreve: n., sheriff, 359 (O.E. scir — refa).
shiten: v., defiled, foul, filthy, 504 (O.E. sciten).
sho: n., shoe, or perhaps sou, a coin. (O.E. scoh).
shoes: n., shoes, 457 (O.E. scohes).
sholde: v., see **shal.**
shoon: v., see **shynen.**
short: adj., short, 93 (O.E. sceort).
shorte: v., shorten, 791 (O.E. sceortian).
shortly: adv., in brief, in a few words, 30 (O.E. sceort + lice).
short-sholdred: adj., thick-set, short-necked, 549 (O.E. sceort + sculdor + ed).
shour: n., shower, 1 (O.E. scur).
shryven: v., shrive, absolve, 226 (O.E. scrifan).
shulder: n., shoulder, 678 (O.E. sculdor).
shynen: v., shine; past tense, **shoon,** 198.
signe: n., sign, token, 226 (O.F. signe).
sike: adj., see **seek.**
sikerly: adv., surely, certainly, 137.
siknesse: n., sickness, illness, 493.
simple: adj., modest, 119 (O.F. simple).

singen: v., sing, 236; past sing., **song,** 122; p.p., **songe,** 266 (O.E. singen).
sinne: n., sin, wicked conduct, 561 (O.E. synn).
sire: n., master, sir, 355.
sitten: v., sit, 94; past tense, **sat,** 469; pres. part., **sittynge,** 633 (O.E. sitten).
sleen: v., slay, kill, 661; p.p., **slayn,** 63 (O.E. slean).
sleighte: n., cunning, trickery, craft, 98 (O.N. slægo).
slepen: v., sleep; pl. pres., **slepen,** 10; past sing., **sleep,** 397 (O.E. slæpan).
sleves: n., sleeves, 93 (O.E. sliefe).
smal: adj., small, little, fine, 9 (O.E. smæl).
smerte: adv., smartly, 149 (O.E. smearte).
smerten: v., smart, sting, hurt, 230; subj. pres., **smerte,** 534 (O.E. smeortan).
smothe: adj., smooth, 690 (O.E. smop).
smothe: adv., smoothly, 676 (O.E. smope).
smylyng: n., smiling, 119 (? M.H.G. smilen + O.E. yng).
snewen: v., snow, abound, 345 (O.E. sniwan).
snybben: v., reprove, reprimand, snub, 523 (O.N. snubba).
sobrely, adv., demurely, sedately, soberly, 289 (O.F. sobre + lice).
softe: adj., soft, 153 (O.E. softe).
solaas: n., cheer, amusement, pleasure, 798 (O.F. solas).
solempne: adj., pompous, important, festive, 209. See note (O.F. solempne).
solempnely: adv., pompously, 274 (O.F. solempne + O.E. lice).
som: adj., some, a certain, 640 (O.E. sum).
somdel: adv., somewhat, a little, 174 (O.E. sum + dæl).
somer: n., summer, 394 (O.E. sumor).
somnour: n., summoner (O.F. sumenour).
somtyme: adv., formerly, once, 65 (O.E. sum + tima).
somwhat: adv., a little, 264 (O.E. sum + hwæt).
sondry: adj., sundry, different, various, 14 (O.E. syndrig).
sone: n., son, 79 (O.E. sunn).
song: n., song, anthem, 711 (O.E. sang).
song: v., see **singen.**
sonne: n., sun, 7 (O.E. sunne).
soo, so: adv., in this manner, 102, 807 (O.E. swa).
soore: adv., sorely, bitterly, 148 (O.E. sare).
soote: adj., sweet, 1 (O.E. swot).
sooth: n., truth, 284 (O.E. sod).
soothly: adv., truly, candidly, 117 (O.E. so lice).
sop: n, sop, soaked bread, 334 (O.E. sopa).
soper: n., super, 348 (O.F. soper).
sort: n., lot, destiny, fate, 844 (O.F. sorte).
sothe: n., truth, 283 (O.E. soo).
soule: n., soul, 301 (O.E. sawol).
soun: n., sound, 674 (O.F. son).
sounynge: v., sounding, talking loudly about proclaiming, resounding, 275. (O.F. suner).
souple: adj., supple, soft, pliable, 203 (O.F. souple).
sovereyn: adj., ver yhigh, supreme, 67 (O.F. soverain).
sowe: n., sow, pig, 552 (O.E. sugn).
sowen: v., sow; p.p., **sowed,** 685 (O.E. seowian).
sownen: v., sound, 565 (O.E. suner).
space: n., opportunity, 35; space of time, 87; course, 176 (O.F. espace).
spade: n., spade, 553 (O.E. spadn).
spak: v., see **speken.**
spanne: n., span, eight inches, 155 (O.E. spanne).

sparen: v., spare, shirk, refrain from, 192 (O.E. sparsian).
sparwe: n., sparrow, 626 (O.E. spearwa).
speche: n., speech, language, choice of words, 307 (O.E. spæc).
special: adj., special, 440 (O.F. especial).
specially: adv., in particular, 15 (O.F. especial + ly).
speden: v., prosper, give success, 769 (O.E. spedan).
speken: v., speak, 636; past tense, **spak,** 124 (O.E. specan).
spenden: v., spend, 645 (O.E. spendan).
spere: n., spear, 114 (O.E. spere).
spiced: adj., scrupulous, hypercritical, sophisticated, 526 (O.F. espice).
spore: n., spur, 473 (O.E. spura).
spryngen: v., spring, break, 822 (O.E. spirngan).
squyer: n., squire. See note to 79 (O.F. esquier).
staat: n., state, condition, estate, 716 (O.F. estat).
stable: n., stable, stall, 28 (O.F. stable).
staf: n., staff, stick, 495 (O.E. stæf).
stature: n., stature, height, 83 (O.F. stature).
statut: n., statute, law, 327 (O.F. statut).
stede: n., place, 231 (O.E. stede).
stelen: v., steal, 562 (O.E. stelan).
stemen: v., shine, gleam, 202 (O.E. steman).
stepe: adj., bright, glittering, prominent, 201 (O.E. steap).
sterre: n., star, 268 (O.E. steorra).
stewe: n., fishpond, 350 (O.F. estui).
stif: adj., strong, harsh, 673 (O.E. stif).
stonden: v., stand, be placed, 88; abide by, 778 (O.E. standan).
stoon: n., stone, 699 (O.E. stan).
stoor: n., store, stock of cattle, 598 (O.F. estor).
storie: n., story, 709 (O.F. estoire).
stot: n., nag, cob, 615 (O.E. stot).
stout: adj., stout, strong, 545 (O.F. estout).
straunge: adj., foreign, strange, 13 (O.F. estrange).
streight: adv., straightway, straight, 671 (O.E. streht).
streit: adj., strict, narrow, 174 (O.F. estreit).
streite: adv., tightly, 457 (O.F. estreite).
strem: n., stream, 464; current, 402 (O.E. stream).
strengthe: n., strength, 84 (O.E. strengo).
strike: n., hank of flax, 676 (O.E. strica).
stronde: n., shore, strand, 13 (O.E. strond).
studie: n., study, learning, 303 (O.F. estudie).
studie: v., study, 184. See note to 841 (O.F. estudier).
styward: n., steward, 579 (O.E. stig + weard).
substaunce: n., possessions, personal property, 489 (O.F. substance).
subtilly: adv., craftily, cunningly, 610 (O.F. sutil).
suffisaunce: n., sufficiency, 490 (O.F. suffisance).
superfluitee: n., excess, superfluity, 436 (O.F. superfluité).
surcote: n., over-coat, coat worn over another, surcoat, 617 (O.F. sur + cote).
surgerye: n., surgery, 413 (O.F. sugerie).
swan: n., swan, 206 (O.E. swan).
swerd: n., sword, 112 (O.E. sweord).
swere: v., swear, affirm, 454; p.p., **swore,** 810 (O.E. swerian).
swete: adj., sweet, fragrant, 5 (O.E. swete).
swetely: adv., pleasantly, 221 (O.E. swete + lice).

swich: adj., such, 3 (O.E. swylc).
swift: adj., swift, rapid, 190 (O.E. swift).
swyn: n., swine, pigs, 598 (O.E. swin).
swynk, swink: n., toil, work, labour, 188 (O.E. swinc).
swynken: v., work, toil, 186 (O.E. swincan).
swynkere: n., toiler, worker, 531 (O.E. swinc + ere).
syde: n., side, 112 (O.E. side).
syn: conj., since, 601 (O.E. sippn).
sythe: n., time, 485 (O.E. sio).

taak: v., see **taken.**
tabard: n., tabard, sleeveless coat worn by a herald, 20; smock, 541 (O.F. tabard).
taffata: n., taffeta, fine silk, 440 (O.F. taffetas).
taille: n., credit, tally, 570. See note (O.F. taillee).
taken: v., take, 34; pres. subj., **take,** 503; impers. sing., **taak,** 789 (O.E. tacan).
takel: n., tackle, archery gear, bows and arrows, 106 (M.L.G. takel).
tale: n., tale, 36 (O.E. tain).
talen: v., tell tales, 772 (O.E. talian).
tapicer: n., upholsterer, tapestry maker, 362 (O.F. tapicier).
tappestere: n., barmaid, 241 (O.E. tæppa + estre).
targe: n., small shield, 471 (O.F. targe).
tart: adj., sharp-tasting, bitter, acid, 381 (O.E. teart).
tartre: n., tartar, 630 (O.F. tartre).
taryynge: n., delay, 821 (O.E. tergan + ung).
taughte: v., see **techen.**
tavernes: n., taverns, 240 (O.F. tavern).
techen: v., teach, 308; past tense, **taughte,** 497; p.p., **y-taught,** 127 (O.E. tæcan).
techyng: n., teaching, 518 (O.E. tæcan + ung).
tellen: v., tell, relate, 38 (O.E. tellan).
tempest: n., storm, 406 (O.F. tempeste).
temple: n., inn of court, temple, 567 (O.F. temple).
tendre: adj., tender, pitiful, piteous, 7 (O.F. tendre).
terme: n., legal phraseology, precise terms, 323 (O.F. terme).
text: n., authority, quotation, saying, 177 (O.F. texte).
teyen: v., tie; p.p. **teyd.**
than, thanne: adv., then, 12 (O.E. ponne); **than:** conj., than, 322 (O.E. ponne).
thank: n., thank you, acknowledgement, 612 (O.E. panc).
tharray: n., see **array.**
thencrees: n., see **encrees.**
ther: adv., there, 43 (O.E. pær).
theras: adv., where, 172 (O.E. pær — ealswa).
therfore: adv., for that purpose, therefore, 809 (O.E. pær + fore).
therfore: conj., therefore, 189 (O.E. pær + fore).
therof: adv., concerning that matter, 462 (O.E. pær + of).
theron: adv., thereupon, 160 (O.E. pær + on).
therto: adv., moreover, 48 (O.E. pær + to).
therupon: adv., thereupon, 819 (O.E. pær + up + on).
therwith: adv., by means thereof, 678 (O.E. pær + wio).
therwithal: adv., by means thereof, 566 (O.E. pær + wio + eal).
thikke: adj., thick-set, 549 (O.E. picce).

thilke: adj., this same, 182. See **ilke** (O.E. pylc).
thing: n., legal document, 325; thing, obstacle, 276 (O.E. ping).
thinken: v., think of, 346 (O.E. pencan).
thinken: v., impersonal, seem, appear; **thinketh:** it seems, 37; past tense, **thoughte:** it seemed, 385 (O.E. pyncan).
thinne: adj., thin, 679 (O.E. pynne).
thoght: n., thought, 479 (O.E. poht).
thombe: n., thumb. See note to 563 (O.E. puma).
thonder: n., thunder, 492 (O.E. punor).
though: conj., although 68; if, 553 (O.E. peoh).
thoughte: see **thinken.**
thresshen: v., thresh, 536 (O.E. perscan).
thryes: adv., three times, 63 (O.E. pries).
thriftily: adv., carefully, 105 (O.N. prift + ly).
til: prep., to, 180 (O.E. til).
tipet: n., short cape, tippet, 233 (O.E. tæppet).
togidre: adv., together, 824 (O.E. togædre).
tollen: v., take payment, take toll. 562 (O.E. toll).
to-morwe: adv., to-morrow, 780 (O.E. to-morgen).
tonge: n., tongue, 265 (O.E. tunge).
tope: n., top, head, 590 (O.E. top).
toun: n., town, district, village, 217 (O.E. tun).
trappe: n., snare, trap, 145 (O.E. træppe).
tretys: adj., long, well-shaped, 152 (O.F. tretis).
trewe: adj., true, honest, faithful, 531 (O.E. treowe).
trewely: adv., faithfully, honestly, 481; certainly, indeed, 761 (O.E. treowe + lice).
trompe: n., trumpet, 674 (O.F. trompe).
trouthe: n., truth, loyalty, 46 (O.E. treowd).
trowen: v., believe, should say, 155 (O.E. treowan).
trussen: v., pack, 681 (O.F. trusser).
tukken: v., tuck up (O.E. tucian).
twelf: adj., twelve, 651 (O.E. twelf).
tweye: adj., twain, two, 704 (O.E. twegan).
twinne: v., depart, 835 (O.E. twinne).
tyde: n., tide, 401 (O.E. tid).
tyme: n., time, 35 (O.E. tima).
tythes: n., tithes, a tax of one-tenth of the produce of the land, 486 (O.E. teooa).

undergrowe: adj., undersized, short of stature, 156 (O.E. under + growen).
understonden: v., understand, 746 (O.E. under + stonden).
undertake: v., affirm, am sure, dare say, vow, undertake, 288 (O.E. under + tacan).
unknowe: adj., unknown, 126 (O.E. un + knowen).
untrewe: adv., incorrectly, untruly, untruthfully, 735 (O.E. un + treowe).
usage: n., practice, use, custom, 110 (O.F. usage).

vavasour: n., sub-vassal, vassal of a vassal, 360 (O.F. vavassour).
venerye: n., hunting, 166 (O.F. venerie).
verdit: n., verdict, decision, 787 (O.F. verdit).
vernicle: n., vernicle. See note to 685 (O.F. veronicle).
verraily: adv., truly, indeed, 338 (O.F. verrai + ly).

verray: adj., true, 72. See note (O.F. verrai).
vertu: n., power to produce, vitalising power, 4 (O.F. vertu).
vertuous: adj., capable, respectable, well-to-do, 251 (O.F. vertuous).
veyl: n., veil, 695 (O.F. veill).
veyne: n., vein of a plant, 3 (O.F. veine).
viage: n., journey, expedition, voyage, 77 (O.F. viage).
vigilies: n., vigils, meetings on the eve of a festival, 377 (O.F. vigile).
vileynye: n., any conduct unbecoming a knight, unseemly behaviour, lack of breeding, ungentlemanly speech, 70 (O.F. vilenie).
visage: n., face, 109 (O.F. visage).
vitaille: n., victuals, provisions, 248 (O.F. vitaille).
vouche-sauf: v., grant, permit, 812 (O.F. voucher + O.F. sauf).
voys: n., voice, 688 (O.F. vois).

waiten: v., look, set store by, require, be cautious, 525 (O.F. waiter).
walet: n., wallet, 681 (Ety. dub.).
wan: v., see **winnen.**
wandrynge: n., travelling, 467 (O.E. wandrian).
wantown: adj., gay, uncontrolled, carefree, 208 (O.E. wan + O.E. togen).
wantownesse: n., freak, affectation, 265 (O.E. wan + O.E. togen + O.E. nesse).
war: adj., aware, prudent, wary, 157 (O.E. wær).
wastel breed: n., choice bread (O.F. gastel + O.E. bread).
waterless: adj., without water, out of water, 180 (O.E. wæter + O.E. leas).
wateryng: n., place where horses were watered, 826 (O.E. wæter + O.E. ung).
webbe: n., weaver, 362 (O.E. webba).
weep: v., see **wepen.**
weel: adv., see **wel.**
wel: adv., well, 29, some, 24 (O.E. wel).
welcome: adj., welcome, 762 (O.E. wel + cuman).
wenden: v., go, journey, 21; past tense, **wente,** 78 (O.E. wendan).
wepen: v., weep, 144; past tense, **weep,** 148 (O.E. wepan).
wepynge: n., weeping, 231 (O.E. wepan + ung).
were, weren: v., see **been.**
were: v., wear, 75 (O.E. werian).
werk: n., work, 479 (O.E. weorc).
werken: v., work, act, 779; past tense, **wroghte,** 497; p.p., **wroght,** 196 (O.E. wyrcan).
werre: n., war, 47 (O.F. werre).
werte: n., wart, 555 (O.E. wearte).
west: n., west country, 388 (O.E. west).
wetten: v., wet, 129 (O.E. wætan).
wex: n., wax, 675 (O.E. weax).
wey: n., way, route, journey, road, 34 (O.E. weg).
weyen: v., weigh; past tense, **weyede,** 454 (O.E. wegan).
whan; conj., when, 1 (O.E. hwænne).
what: pron., what, what sort of a? 40 (O.E. hwæt).
what: adv., why? 184 (O.E. hwæt).
whelke: n., pimple, spot, 632 (O.E. hwylca).
whelpe: n., puppy, cub, 257 (O.E. hwelp).
wher-with: adv., whereby, means with which, 302 (O.E. hwær + O.E. wiþ).
which: pron., which? whom? of what sort? 40 (O.E. hwilc).

whil: conj., while, 35 (O.E. hwil).
whilom: adv., formerly, once, 795 (O.E. hwilum).
whistlynge: adj., whistling, 170 (O.E. hwistlian).
whit: adj., white, 90 (O.E. hwit).
widwe: n., widow, 253 (O.E. widwe).
wight: n., person, man, 71 (O.E. wiht).
willen: v., will, desire, intend, 42; pres. tense, **wol;** past, **wolde(n)** (O.E. willan).
winnen: v., win, gain; past tense, **wan,** 442; p.p., **wonne,** 51 (O.E. winnan).
winning: n., winnings, gain, profit, 275 (O.E. winnan + ung).
wisdom: n., wisdom, knowledge, learning, 371 (O.E. wis + O.E. dom).
wit: n., intelligence, 574 (O.E. witt).
witen: v., know; pres. sing., **wot, woot,** 389; pres, pl., **woot,** 740; past sing., **wiste,** 224 (O.E. witan).
withalle: adv., withal, moreover, 127 (O.E. wip + alle).
withholden: v., retain, 511 (O.E. wiohealdan).
withouten: prep., without, not counting, excluding, 461 (O.E. wioutan).
withseyen: v., gainsay, contradict, oppose, 805 (O.E. wio + secgan).
wo: n., sorrow, trouble, woe, 351 (O.E. wea).
wol: v., see **willen.**
wolden: v., see **willen.**
womman: n., women, 459 (O.E. wif + mann).
wonder: adj., wondrous, wonderfully, 483 (O.E. wundor).
wonder: n., wonder, marvel, 402 (O.E. wundor).
wonderly: adv., wonderfully, unusually, remarkably, 84 (O.E. wundor + ly).
wone: n., wont, custom, habit, 335 (O.E. wuna).
wonen: v., dwell; pres. part., **wonynge,** 388 (O.E. wunian).
wonyng: n., dwelling, house, 606 (O.E. wunnung).
wood: adj., mad, 184 (O.E. wod).
woodecraft: n., forestry, hunting, 110 (O.E. wiodu + O.E. cræft).
worldly: adj., worldly, 292. See note (O.E. woruldlic).
worstede: n., worsted, a kind of wool, 262 (O.E. wuroestede).
worth: adj., worth, 182; worthwhile, 785 (O.E. weorpe).
worthy: adj., distinguished, respectable, well-to-do, 43 (O.E. weorpig).
worthinesse: n., distinction, prowess, 50 (O.E. weorpig + nesse).
wrastlynge: n., wrestling match, 548 (O.E. wræstliung).
wrighte: n., workman, 614 (O.E. wyrhta).
writ: n., what is written, the Scriptures, 739 (O.E. writ).
writen: v., write, 96 (O.E. wryten).
wroght: v., see **werken.**
wrooth: adj., angry, 451 (O.E. wrap).
wyd: adj., wide, scattered, spacious, 28 (O.E. wid).
wyf: n., woman, wife, 234 (O.E. wyf).
wympel: n., wimple, a covering for the neck, 151. See note (O.E. wimpel).
wyn: n., wine, 334 (O.E. win).
wynnen: v., see **winnen.**
wypen: v., wipe; past sing., **wyped,** 133 (O.E. wipian).
wys: adj., discreet, prudent, wise, 68 (O.E. wise).

y-: a suffix often used for the past participle (O.E. ge-).
yaf: v., see **yeve.**
y-bore: v., see **bere.**
y-cleped: v., see **clepen.**

y-come: see **comen.**
ye: n., eye, 10 (O.E. eage).
ye: pron., you, 769; at. and acc., **yow,** 34 (O.E. ge).
yeddynges: n., songs, ballads, 237. See note (O.E. giddung).
yeer: n., year, years, 82 (O.E. gear).
yeldhalle: n., guildhall, hall belonging to a guild, 370 (O.E. gield + heall).
yeldynge: n., yield, produce, 596 (O.E. gieldung).
yelow: adj., yellow, 675 (O.E. geolu).
yeman: n., yeoman, 101 (O.E. geman).
yemanly: adv., in yeomanlike fashion, as a yeoman should, 106 (O.E. geman + lice).
yerde: n., yardstick, rod, 149 (O.E. gierd).
yet: adv., yet, nevertheless, 255 (O.E. giet).
yeven: v., give, 177; past tense, **yaf,** 227 (O.E. giefan).
y-falle: v., see **fallen.**
y-go: see **goon.**
y-knowe: see **knowen.**
y-lad: see **leden.**
y-lyk: adj., like, 592 (O.E. gelic).
ymage: n., image, 418. See note to 411 (O.F. image).
ynogh: adj., enough, 373 (O.E. genoh).
yong: adj., young, 7 (O.E. geong).
yow: see **ye.**
y-punysshed: see **punysshe.**
y-preved: see **proven.**
y-purfiled: see **purfile.**
y-ronne: see **rennen.**
y-sene: see **sene.**
y-shadwed: see **shadwen.**
y-shave: see **shaven.**
y-shorn: see **sheren.**
y-shrive: see **shryven.**
y-taught: see **techen.**
y-teyd: see **teyen.**
y-wroght: see **werken.**
y-wympled: p.p., see **wympul.**